CREDO
INTERNATIONAL

Voices of Religious Liberalism
From Around the World

CREDO
INTERNATIONAL

HUMANUNITY PRESS
703 Stratford Court #11
Del Mar, CA 92014
Donmitzimac@aol.com

*This book is available in quantity at special
discounts for your group or organization
by contacting the author.*

*US - $17.00
CAN - $26.00
UK - £10.50
EU - 18.00
AUS - $30.00*

ISBN: 0-9726236-0-4

Cover Design by Mitzi

This Book is Dedicated to

Rev. Polly Guild

and
The International Council of
Unitarians and Universalists

From All Who Dwell Below the Skies
Let Faith and Hope with Love Arise.
Let Beauty, Truth and Good Be Sung,
Through Every Land by Every Tongue.

FOREWORD AND ACKNOWLEDGEMENTS

Three years ago I published CREDO, which presented the personal stories of thirty-seven prominent Unitarians and Universalists from the past. All but two of these were from the United States.

As I explained at that time, it is a practice of the First Unitarian Universalist Church in San Diego, where I am a member, to periodically have congregants share in public worship their own spiritual odysseys, affirmations, motivating beliefs. I have never failed to be deeply moved and inspired by these revealing declarations.

Wishing it possible to hear such luminaries as Channing, Parker, Clara Barton, Susan B. Anthony and others present their own Credos, I decided the only way that could be done was if I researched their lives and recreated what I perceived they might say had they appeared at our services some Sunday morning.

The success of that book prompted the Rev. Polly Guild, volunteer Program Director of the International Council of Unitarians and Universalists, to suggest the writing of a second volume featuring founders and leaders of these progressive religious movements around the world. This compilation is the result of my eager response to her recommendation.

The original book stimulated many to ask: Why do you call it CREDO? Are we not a movement that renounces Creeds? Isn't the title an oxymoron? Assuming that this new volume will prompt the same question, I offer this three-part explanation.

First, as Tom Owen-Towle, minister emeritus in San Diego, has written: "The Latin word 'Credo' does not translate as 'I believe,' which usually halts with intellectual assent. No, the term Credo refers to something thicker and profounder: 'I give my heart and loyalty to . . .'." I use the word in that sense. Not just as a statement of belief, but as an affirmation of those fundamental loyalties of one's life.

Second, even if you choose to apply the most limited definition of Credo, to simply mean "I believe," note that it is singular, not plural. Each of us have our own beliefs, but we do not require that they be shared by others. It is "I believe," not "We believe."

Thirdly, beliefs do not exist without actions. What people do is the true expression of what they genuinely believe. That is why a significant portion of the Credos presented in this book are recitations of activities to which these persons dedicated their lives, a celebration of the causes to which they were committed.

Another question sure to be asked is: How did you decide who would be included in the volume?

Primarily, I relied on the recommendations received from key persons in the respective countries. The majority of those I chose to include are here because the International Council of Unitarians and Universalists' correspondent in his or her nation nominated them.

Elsewhere, as from the United Kingdom and Canada, where there were so many who merited inclusion, I sought a balance between men and women, clergy and laity, famous and relatively unknown, historical to near-contemporary. In so doing it was necessary to leave out many who rightfully belong in a collection of this kind.

Since my earlier book focused primarily on well-known figures from the U.S.A., I included only three this time. George de Benneville and John Murray are here because they brought Universalism to the United States from Europe and I wanted to indicate the linkage from nation to nation. Judith Sargent Murray is here simply because I found her such a remarkable person that I couldn't leave her out.

Every effort has been made to be as factually accurate as possible. This has not always been a simple matter since there are often differences on details in separate resource materials. These discrepancies, however, always seemed to be relatively insignificant.

As well, I have made a sincere attempt to allow the "speaker" to present himself or herself in a way which I perceived to be expressive of the individual personality. Wherever possible I have used the speaker's own words, paraphrasing only when it seemed necessary.

Of course, there are also some flights of fancy on my part. I would not want you to believe that Catherine Helen Spence referred you to her Internet Home Page to see a list of her publications, or that Joseph Priestley asked you to remember him whenever you drink a soda. Please grant me the privilege of a bit of whimsy.

One of the true joys of preparing this book was the opportunity of making friends with kindred souls on six continents. I could never have compiled this material without the help of Mark Allstrom in Australia, Ladislav Pivec in the Czech Republic, Lene Lund Shoemaker in Denmark, Wolfgang Jantz in Germany, Olga Flores in Bolivia, Andrew Hill in the United Kingdom, Indirius Dominic Bhatti in Pakistan, Rebecca Quimada-Sienes in the Philippines, Czeslaw Glogowski in Poland, Gordon Oliver in South Africa, Jaume de Marcos Andreu in Spain, Paulo Ereno in Brazil, Shigeo Akashi in Japan, and translator Tomoko Miura. My heartfelt thanks to each of you.

I wish, also, to acknowledge and express gratitude to the authors of other sources from which most of this material has come. I make no claim of being an original scholar. I have not personally searched the dusty archives of our past. Rather, I have trusted the scholarship of those who have these abilities and inclinations.

Because these individual chapters are prepared as if they were oral presentations I have not attempted footnotes as would have been required in another kind of manuscript. I do wish to include, however, the primary sources from which this material was gleaned. That list appears on the back pages.

So, read and enjoy. I hope you will be both enlightened and entertained. Perhaps it will be your good fortune to have some of these fascinating people appear at your services some Sunday morning and share these stories with you in person. That is what happened in many congregations across America after the original CREDO was published. Maybe it will be an international phenomenon this time.

Don McEvoy

TABLE OF CONTENTS

Salve! Greetings! My name is

ARIUS

It is commonly said that I was the first Unitarian, but I must take issue with that claim. To be sure, as a presbyter of the Church in Alexandria in the fourth century of the Common Era, I taught that God was One and Eternal and that Jesus was a created being and thus not God—or part of the Godhead was the way theologians put it.

I did not consider this a radical idea. I am confident that this was exactly what Jesus' early disciples thought about him. Some probably saw him as the long-awaited Jewish Messiah. Others may have seen him as a great prophet in the tradition of the Hebrew prophets. Some apparently thought he would be a secular leader who would overthrow Caesar and bring an end to the Roman occupation of Palestine. But there is no evidence in Scripture that any of them believed him to be God.

This point of view, while shared by many in my time, was not the prevailing belief of the majority of my fellow priests across the Empire. I had come to my conclusions based on my reading of Scripture and study with Lucian, the bishop of Antioch. I held Jesus in highest esteem and honored him as the fullest revelation of God available to humankind, but not God Himself. This was not enough for those who branded those of us who felt this way as heretics. My response was that those who taught that Jesus was God were really the heretics, since they had no basis in Scripture.

But I am getting ahead of my story. Let me go back and start again.

I was born in Libya. The exact date is unknown, but it was about 250 C.E. My study for the priesthood was in Antioch, as I

1

already mentioned. After ordination I was assigned to work in Alexandria, Egypt where I attracted a large and enthusiastic following.

I was an unusually tall man, which drew attention to me. Contemporaries hailed me as a persuasive preacher and teacher who integrated ideas of Neoplatonism, which accented the absolute oneness of the divinity as the highest perfection, with a literal, rationalistic interpretation of Christian Scripture.

Opponents said that I was overly argumentative and confrontational, but no one ever questioned my integrity or my moral character.

To better explain in detail my disputed teachings, I wrote a book entitled *Thalia* which means Banquet. But these rather dry-as-dust theological concepts were much more effectively distributed throughout the entire Mediterranean world through a most unusual medium. Situated as it was on one of the major trade routes, Alexandria had many travelers and visitors. Troubadors of the Church translated my teachings into popular songs. These were heard by those who passed our way, and spread far and wide by them as they traveled on.

They became so widespread, in fact, that many church leaders felt threatened. In the year 321 C.E. the bishops of North Africa convened a synod and voted to excommunicate me.

This was hardly the end of the matter. The controversy did not subside, but on the contrary, grew more intense. So contentious did the matter of Arianism (as my position came to be known) become that all of the Bishops of the entire Church were called into a Council in the City of Nicaea in the year 325.

That Council codified the doctrine of the Trinity in a statement that has been known ever since as the Nicaean Creed. Everyone present was required to sign this creedal statement, which, in good conscience, I could not do. Because I refused to put my name on the document, I was once again designated as a heretic and forbidden to engage in any priestly activities.

I suppose they thought this would bring closure to the Arian Controversy, but it was not to be. Even though I had been sent into exile and forbidden to speak, many others continued to preach as I had done.

But there were other considerations which transcended the theological and ecclesiastical. As seems to have been the case throughout human history, religious matters were intertwined with politics.

Twelve years after I was banished the Emperor Constantine died and was succeeded in the Eastern part of the Empire by Constantius II who was sympathetic to me and those who believed as I did. Through the intervention of his daughter, Constantia, I was permitted to return from exile, and my doctrines were once again openly taught. Two years later I died on the streets of Constantinople.

But Constans, who sided with the orthodox churchmen, was Emperor in the West. The division of the Empire between Rome and Constantinople mirrored the division of opinion in the church. People lined up on one side or the other more to curry approval of the secular rulers than as a reflection of their religious convictions.

After Constantius' death in 361 the empire consolidated. Then, in 381, another Council was convened, this time in Constantinople. Once again, the Nicaen Creed was reaffirmed and Arianism was condemned.

Nevertheless, Arianism continued among some Germanic tribes to the end of the 7th century. In more modern times many Unitarians were, and are, virtual Arians.

And this may surprise many of you. Not only have I been honored as a herald of the Unitarian Church, but also of the Jehovah's Witnesses. Their "Christology," that is, concept of Christ, is a form of Arianism. They regard me a forerunner of Charles Taze Russell who founded this group in the late 19th century.

Buenos Dias. I am

MIGUEL SERVETUS VILLANOVUS

If you have heard of me at all it was probably simply as Servetus.

I was born in Huesca, Spain in the year 1511. Even though that was a century before the Spanish novelist Cervantes created Don Quixote, there was much about my life and personality which seemed to mirror that romantic knight who dreamed glorious dreams and tilted at windmills. Perhaps those are right who say that every Spaniard has something of Don Quixote in him.

After an uneventful childhood I went to Toulouse to study law. While there I developed an interest in theology and the study of the Bible. As a Catholic in Spain I had no personal access to Scripture. It was interpreted for us by the priests. So this was a new and exciting experience for me. Gutenberg had published the Bible with his new invention of movable type only a few years earlier.

As I read the Bible I was astounded to discover that the doctrine of the Trinity, that is, the three co-equal persons in the Godhead—Father, Son and Holy Spirit—was nowhere mentioned in Scripture. This was quite a revelation to me since this doctrine was so prominent in the teachings of the church I had known since childhood.

Even with my growing skepticism about the authenticity of the church's teaching, I left Toulouse and took a position as secretary to the priest who was Charles V's confessor in Italy. While there I secretly studied the writings of the leaders of the Protestant Reformation which was raging throughout Europe. Little by little, I became convinced that the Reformers like Luther, Zwingli, and Calvin were not revolutionary enough.

They sought to correct some of the most obvious vices of the Catholic Church, but were not interested in tackling the more serious matters such as the error of the Council of Nicaea which formulated the doctrine of the Trinity. This was an idea which was totally incompatible with the unity of the divine nature of God.

I began to express these kinds of ideas among those I thought were close friends, but soon found myself under investigation by the Inquisition. It was time for me to leave Italy and move on. I set out to visit the leaders of the Reformation, certain that I would be able to convince them of the errors of their ways. On the contrary, I met resistance that ranged from Luther's indifference to Zwingli's denunciation of me as "that criminal Spaniard whose false and evil doctrines would sweep away our whole Christian religion."

Failing to impress those so-called leaders, I decided to take my case to the masses. At age 22 I published a book entitled *On the Errors of the Trinity*. Public reaction was so life-threatening that I had to move on again. This time I went to Paris under the alias of Michael de Villeneuve and took a job as a proofreader of medical textbooks. This stimulated me to enter medical school and begin studies to become a physician. But I quickly became aware that my professors were teaching false theories and felt it necessary to organize classes on my own where I instructed my fellow students on the errors of orthodox medicine. Very shortly thereafter I was banished again.

This time I moved to Vienna where I was able to convince the Archbishop to employ me as his personal physician, still using the name Michael de Villeneuve. For several years I conducted myself with discretion and found safety behind this disguise.

But after John Calvin, whom I had known briefly in my student days, rose to his position of preeminence in Geneva, I could constrain myself no longer. I began a correspondence with him, though carefully hiding behind my assumed name. For a while the correspondence was civil as we debated various theological issues. Then he sent me a copy of his book, *Institutio*, which I returned with all his obvious errors notated in the margins. He responded with a vicious diatribe, ending our correspondence by saying he "cared as little for your words as I care for the hee-haw of a donkey."

I then wrote and published *Christianismi Restituitio* (The Restoration of Christianity) as an answer and antidote to his book. The publication was done secretly. The book did not even carry the name of an author. I did, however, foolishly or not, add the initials MSV over the date of publication. Calvin immediately recognized these as Miguel Servetus Villanovus and set out to destroy me.

He went about it in an incredible way. He reported me to the Inquisition! Can you imagine? The arch-enemy of the Catholic Church using the investigative office of that church to eliminate an enemy of his own! But that is what he did. He turned over all my letters to the Inquisition. I was arrested, tried, and condemned to be burned to death.

On the day I was to be executed, after the firewood had already been stacked around the stake, my guards permitted me to take a walk alone in the prison yard. All they later found was the ladder I used to scale the prison wall. They went on with the ceremony, however, as I was burned in effigy along with all my books and papers.

I set out immediately for Geneva. In retrospect I can see that was probably an ill-advised and quixotic thing to do. Still, I was determined to confront Calvin face-to-face. On the first Sunday after my arrival there I went to the cathedral where he was preaching. I was spotted in the congregation and was arrested and in chains within an hour.

It did not matter that I was a Spaniard and not subject to Genevese jurisdiction, nor that it was illegal for a clergyman to order an arrest and imprisonment when no charges had been filed or trial held. This was John Calvin's Geneva, and he had assumed almost total dictatorial control. He did, however, have to make some concessions to civil law.

Unlike the Inquisition which rewarded informers by giving them a portion of the property and resources of persons condemned for heresy, Genevese civil law decreed that those making charges were to be jailed at the same time as those whom they accused. If the charges were upheld in court the accuser was freed, but if they were proven false the accuser faced additional incarceration. Calvin, of course, would take no such chances. Therefore, he assigned his cook the dubious responsibility of filing an indictment of 23 charges against me. The poor cook went dutifully off to jail.

Calvin himself took over the prosecution and told all manner of lies about me. At first I tried to maintain a calm demeanor and respond with reserved logic. But under such extreme provocation I could not continue in that manner.

Finally, one day in open court I screamed at Calvin: "You lied. You lied, ignorant calumniator that you are. Wrath boils up within you when you are hounding anyone to death. Would that all your magic were still hidden away in your mother's womb so that I could have a chance to recount your errors."

Then, turning to the judge, I cried: "I am not the one who should be on trial. You should not only find him guilty and sentence him, but should banish him from your city."

There was never any doubt what the verdict would be. I was found guilty of heresy and sentenced to be burned to death on the following day.

Calvin did not attend my public burning, but at the cathedral the following Sunday he boasted that justice had been done and God's Word glorified as the heretic had been devoured in the holy flames.

Buon Giorno! I am

FAUSTUS SOCINUS

I was born in the year 1539 in the university town of Sienna, near Florence. That is now Italy, of course, but at that time was the Kingdom of Sienna.

When I was three years old Pope Paul III established the Holy Office of the Inquisition to deal with the Protestant Reformation which began in 1517 when Martin Luther nailed his 95 thesis to the door of the castle church in Wittenberg. I mention this to help you get me placed in an historical frame of reference. Also because the Inquisition played such a critical role in my life.

My family was prominent in law and literature and my childhood years were pleasant and privileged. This despite the fact that my father died when I was quite young, and I was raised by my mother and grandmother. The principal male figure in my life was an uncle, Laelius. He was a highly respected theologian, who developed many of the ideas and beliefs which I adopted as my own.

Laelius was committed to the Reformation and traveled often to confer with leaders such as Luther, Zwingli, and Calvin. He made a clean break with Calvin, however, after the execution of Servetus. That was an atrocity which distressed him deeply. Particularly since he knew he held many of the same anti-Trinitarian beliefs for which the martyr had been put to death.

It was my uncle's reputation more than anything which I had said or done that brought me to the attention of the Inquisition when I was only 20 years of age. Knowing I was under investigation, I fled to Zurich for safety. It was there I came into possession of all my uncle's papers and accepted his heretical ideas for myself.

Three years later I anonymously published my first book. It was a prologue to the Gospel of John in which I outlined my belief that the Trinity was false doctrine without Scriptural basis. I wrote that Jesus was not God and his divinity derived by "office" rather than "nature." In other words, Jesus was human, fully human, but achieved divinity by voluntarily accepting God's will for his life. But he was not an intrinsic part of the Godhead.

Having done that, for some reason I cannot explain, I returned to Florence and became secretary to Isabella, sister of the Grand Duke of Tuscanny. I spent the next twelve years in that position. Basically, I kept my mouth shut and did nothing to arouse the suspicions of the Inquisition. Then, with the Duke's blessing, I left to pursue my true vocation. For the rest of my life I looked back on this period as wasted years.

Heretics were being hunted down and killed all over Europe by both the Catholic Church and the various branches of the Reformation. The only safe havens seemed to be Poland and neighboring Transylvania.

I chose to go to Crackow, Poland where an anti-Trinitarian church had already been established. In 1565 the Polish Reformed Church had split into two distinct bodies. The Major Reformed group believed in the Trinity. The Minor Reformed Church did not.

I emphasize this in order to keep the record straight. Many have credited me with establishing the Unitarian movement in Poland, but that is not so. Than honor belongs to my fellow Italian Georgio Biandrata. I did, however, quickly become the intellectual and spiritual leader of that courageous band of believers.

Surprisingly, even though I was their acknowledged leader, and those who followed my teachings were commonly called "Socinians," I never officially joined their church. Their rules required that I be re-baptized as an adult, and I saw no reason to do so. Therefore, I never joined.

At one time I was invited by King John Sigismund to visit Transylvania and debate certain issues with Francis David, the leader of the Unitarians there. Our debate focused on whether it was proper to address prayers to Jesus. My position was that even though Jesus was not God, he was worthy of adoration by virtue of his adoption as Son of the Father. David, to the contrary, remained unconvinced saying that it should not be done since it was not specifically commanded in Scripture. This unreconciled difference of opinion did nothing to diminish our mutual respect.

During these years I wrote extensively. In addition to many commentaries about God as a unitary being, I also emphasized His loving nature. I rejected completely the idea that God had required the death of Jesus as a pre-condition of forgiveness for a sinful humankind. That seemed to me to be a scandalous libel against a loving Father. Needless to say, I railed against the Calvinistic doctrine of pre-destination.

Having been influenced by the Anabaptists, I preached against war and the bearing of arms. While encouraging Christians to refuse to engage in warfare, I always made it clear that they had an obligation to obey civil authority at all times other than when they were in conflict with the teachings of Jesus.

You can well imagine that many of these ideas were quite controversial and the cause of considerable opposition. Once when I was confined to bed with an illness, a group of students burst in and violently attacked me. They ransacked my house and burned my books and papers. They would surely have killed me had it not been for the fortuitous arrival of a friend who dropped by to visit.

After this event I chose to leave Crackow. I moved to the estate of a wealthy nobleman whose daughter I married. Tragically, within a year she died giving birth to our child. I was left desolate and in despair.

Shortly thereafter the Inquisition moved against my father-in-law. He was charged with having shared my heretical beliefs. The real reason, however, was that his considerable wealth could be confiscated by the Church and his accusers.

I sought refuge once again. This time in the village of Luciawice. There I set myself feverishly to the task of completing my last book, *Christianae Religionis Instituto*, but died before it was finished.

After my death my followers collected my writings into a manuscript called the *Racovian Cathechism*. This document later inspired John Biddle to establish Unitarianism in England.

Thus my influence continued through Biddle to England and on through Joseph Priestley and others to America. This, even though the church in Poland came under relentless opposition from the agents of the Counter Reformation. Within a century of my death almost all the Socinians, later called Unitarians, had been banished or killed.

Dzien Dobry. Ja jestem

SAMUEL PRZYPKOWSKI

I was among those called the Polish Brethren who inherited the legacy of Faustus Socinus and his Unitarian beliefs.

My life covered the years from 1592 to 1670, which was the period of the Counter Reformation when the Catholic Church was attempting to discredit and destroy any, and all, expressions of Protestantism and any others considered by them to be heretical.

We Polish Brethren stood outside the mainstream of the Reformation, of course. Luther and Calvin and Zwingli were just as vociferous in their condemnations of us, but it was the Catholics—particularly the Jesuits—who directly confronted us in Poland.

Among the terms used to describe us were: "rabid dogs," "serpents," "the devil incarnate" and "stinking rabble." One hostile pamphlet, published in 1615, said that "heretics are a special type of beast" . . . and that "to allow freedom of conscience is a diabolic concept."

In response to such as that, I published my own pamphlet in which I sought to demonstrate the absurdity of intolerance among Christians and appealed for mutual love regardless of doctrinal differences. We must not, I wrote, impose spiritual censure on anybody, for each of us has the right to his own individual evaluation. We do not grant anyone the liberty to violate, in private or in public, the freedom of conscience, nor the liberty to propagate religion by force or violence.

Among the fundamental beliefs which I consistently stressed were:

1. The right of dissent is the fundamental right in a Republic composed of persons of many nations and various religions that need tolerance, equality and peace.

2. Freedom of conscience is the foundation of liberty. There is no liberty without the guarantee that people can do what they consider useful and needful without fear of persecution or punishment. Everyone has the right to choose one's own way to salvation.

3. The freedom of conscience guaranteed by the Statutes of 1573, and affirmed in the oath taken by a Polish King at his coronation, works to the benefit of all religious groups. The freedom to practice and to promote one's own faith without interference from either the Church or the State permits all faiths to flourish and to grow.

I may have been the first person in history to enunciate the concept of the complete separation of Church and State. Just as one should not mix together matters of religion with matters of state, neither should one allow religion and state to be in opposition to one another.

The two, Church and State, are completely different entities and neither should encroach on the province of the other. Each must agree to mutual limits which keep it from intruding into the sphere of the other. When the State with compulsory authority encroaches on the government of the Church, or when the Church takes the sword out of hands of the civil authority, there is a violation of justice.

These kingdoms are different in kind. There is a spiritual one without compulsion, and a secular one with coercive authority. Both must exist in the same nation without conflict of jurisdiction. If both, so separate, remain within their own limits, each may exercise its functions without hindrance.

It was my conviction that it was absurd to exclude any person from political public life because of his religious association.

My criterion for judging people was not the adherence to the invented dogmatic or ritual demands of any church, but to the fulfillment of moral precepts, the living of a principled life.

Those who demand blind belief in the dogmas of their religion and blind obedience to their orders, do so in an attempt to protect their own interests. But in so doing they undercut those very interests. When doctrines cannot be subjected to the test of reason, and followers are told that to accept them without question is virtue, the prelates of the Church are usurping the authority of Christ. The devil himself could not invent anything so mischievous.

We can give up our rights and liberties only in matters which are morally indifferent. Whenever we find anything that influences our behavior and actions and is contrary to reason, it is our sacred obligation to dissent.

Nonetheless, we cannot impose this on others. If they choose to submit themselves like sheep to the assumed authority of some other religious society, we cannot interfere with their freedom of choice.

I am sorry to report, as you already know, that the religious liberty we achieved in Poland in the 16th century survived only until the middle of the 17th. The political leadership changed and violent persecution fell the lot of the Polish Brethren.

Those who were able to do so fled into exile in Holland, Transylvania, and Germany. They carried with them the seeds of a new Unitarian movement which later blossomed in the English-speaking world.

Most of the Polish Brethren, however, were slaughtered and their lands and possessions confiscated.

The arguments which I proposed in behalf of the separate roles of Church and State found later expression in the writings of Voltaire, John Locke, and the English Unitarian Joseph Priestley.

Of greatest significance is that they were heard anew in the writings of James Madison and Thomas Jefferson. That is a heritage in which I take profound satisfaction.

How many Americans, do you think, are aware that their religious freedom is a legacy inherited from the Polish Brethren?

Dzien Dobry. Ja jestem

ANDREW WISZOWATY

My grandfather was Faustus Socinus, who has already told you his story of the establishment of Unitarianism in Poland.

You know, therefore, that even before his death persecution against those who followed his teachings had begun. The years that followed are difficult to describe. For one brief shining period it seemed that toleration would be the way of Poland's future. But it was not to be.

Sympathetic King Sigismund Augustus II died and was replaced by others who were under the influence of the Jesuits and the Counter Reformation. A half-century of violent persecution followed. It was first directed against the larger Protestant Church, but soon turned against the Polish Brethren, the Socinians as well.

When Poland was attacked by the armies of the Protestant King Charles X of Sweden, many Socinians supported the invaders, believing they would be treated more leniently than by their own government.

Although the Swedes came promising stability and peace, their actions belied any such intent. The Polish King, John Casimir, made a solemn vow that if he won back his kingdom he would purge it of heresy, beginning with the traitorous Unitarian Polish Brethren.

He succeeded in driving out the Swedes and carried out his promise with a vengeance. He issued a decree that by July 10, 1660, two years hence, all Unitarians would be stripped of all their lands and possessions, and must either recant or leave Poland.

Persistent attempts were made for many months to negotiate some easing of these extreme measures, but to no avail. Finally, only four months before the fateful final day, the governor of Warsaw permitted us to meet and discuss our religious differences with leaders of the Catholic Church. I was designated as spokesman for the Socinians, facing an array of the ablest disputants the Jesuits could find.

My attempts to convince the King to change his mind fell on deaf ears, even though one of the Catholic debaters said of me: "If all the devils came out of hell they could not defend their religion more strongly than this one man . . . ."

Attempts were made to bribe me to change my position. The governor of Warsaw even offered me a large estate and a generous pension if I would renounce my faith and embrace Catholicism. That, of course, I could not do.

By the time the fateful day arrived all those who could departed, taking with them only their most valued personal possessions. Perhaps one thousand families were left behind in destitution. Most of those who remained were captured and put to death. Only a handful survived for more than a year or two. Twice, during the next two years, I secretly reentered the country to offer solace and support. We covertly convened a synod in 1662 and appointed two ministers to look after the brethren who were in hiding across the land. Sadly, none survived. Socinian Unitarianism died in Poland, but its influence continues to radiate throughout the world.

Those who went into exile scattered in all directions. The larger group, of which I was a part, set out on foot for Transylvania. Another wagon train crossed the Carpathian Mountains where they were attacked by renegade Hungarian soldiers who robbed them of their meager possessions, even stripping the clothes from their bodies and leaving them to die.

Ultimately the survivors found refuge in Silesia, Holstein, Brandenberg, Prussia, Transylvania, and the Rhine Palatinate. In 1663 I moved on to a village on the Rhine near Heidelberg. A small company of the exiles followed me there and for three years we enjoyed relative peace. We were permitted to hold religious services in our homes. But when a number of local residents began to express interest in our views, the Lutheran clergy had laws enacted which forbade the discussion of religious subjects and the distribution of any of our books. We found it necessary to move once again, this time to Holland. I had studied there as a youth, and had many close friends among the Dutch.

Socinian ideas had been introduced to Holland as early as 1598 when two Polish ministers visited the University of Lieden. The authorities denounced them as little better than Mohammedans, burned their books, and exiled them from the country. But the seeds had been planted.

By the time we arrived, two generations later, Socinianism books were widely read. Socinian scholars were included in conversations among those exploring religious ideas. Many were converts-in-waiting.

The Remondstrants had separated from the Reformed Church. Even though there were significant theological differences between them and our small Socinian community, an informal coalition developed between us. They were particularly generous in raising significant sums of money for the relief of Polish Brethren in exile. A generation later they gave liberally for the rebuilding of a fire-razed Unitarian Church in Transylvania.

We built no churches of our own in Holland, but found friendly acceptance with both the Remondstrants and the Mennonites.

The Collegiants provided another area of participation for us. This was not a separate sect, but rather gatherings of lay persons from various churches for prayer, Bible study, and free discussion. Opponents of this movement said that the Collegiants were nothing other than Socinians under an assumed name.

One of the goals which I pursued, and accomplished, was the translation into Dutch of my grandfather's Rakovian Catechism. This became the bridge over which Socianism ideas passed into the Mennonite Church. These two groups had many differences, but much more in common than they had with anyone else in Holland. Both objected to Creeds, took religion directly from the Bible, and emphasized ethical living more than adherence to doctrine.

I realize I have not really told you much about myself, but I thought it more important to spend my time in helping you see the historic connections between the Polish Brethren and the spread of Unitarianism throughout the world.

John Biddle became acquainted with my grandfather's writings and established Unitarianism in England. The Pilgrims who fled Holland before setting sail for the New World were the religious dissidents from whom Unitarianism in America evolved.

It is a glorious history. I am grateful for having been a link in this often bent, but never broken, chain.

Salutations, dear friends. I am

FRANCIS DAVID

I was born in the town of Kolosvar in the country of Transylvania, which is now situated in Romania. I say "now situated" because national borders have shifted many times over the years as empires have waxed and waned, and my country has borne many names. But to me it will be Transylvania forever.

The year of my birth was 1510. You may note this was a mere seven years before the German monk, Martin Luther, shook the foundations of both the ecclesiastical and political landscapes of Europe with the onset of the Protestant Reformation.

In the beginning that movement toward reform had little influence on me. As I grew into young manhood my religious sensibilities were acute and I decided at a very early age that I would enter the Catholic priesthood.

Ironically, I was sent to Wittenberg in Germany for my studies. This was the place where, just a few years earlier, Luther had posted his demands for change on the Cathedral door. Still, I was largely untouched by Lutheran teaching. I just knew that my professors taught me he was a dangerous heretic.

After ordination I returned to Kolosvar and assumed the directorship of a school. On returning I discovered that during my absence the Reformation had taken root in my homeland. I, then, began to take it more seriously.

Thus began an odyssey that took me far beyond anything I could have imagined. I became convinced that the reformers were correct in their assessment of the vices and corruption within the Roman Church. Consequently, I transferred my allegiance to the Lutherans and soon rose to the position of superintendent of my area.

But my ever-inquiring mind kept me in search of evolving truths and challenges. That led to the judgment that Lutheranism had not gone nearly far enough. I saw the changes demanded as being largely superficial. To me, they seemed far short of true reform.

So I made another shift in my loyalties and joined the Calvinist wing of the protest movement. I perceived that the followers of Calvin were more Bible-centered in their doctrines.

As I threw myself into Biblical study however, I found to my dismay that most of the basic tenets of Calvinism had no basis in Holy Scripture. I concluded that the only way to purify the church was to apply reason to the process of Biblical study and to attempt to go back—insofar as that was possible—and recreate the church as it was in the beginning. That is, an assemblage of people seeking to follow the teachings of Jesus. I concluded that the Sermon on the Mount was the essence of Christianity and that those who claimed to be followers of Jesus had to live loving and ethical lives in the service of others.

The teachings of a man named Arius, in the 4th century, inspired me. He taught, according to the Scripture, that Jesus was not a god, but fully a man who lived in obedience to his understanding of God's will. The idea of a Trinity, in which Jesus was one manifestation of God, and the Holy Spirit a third, was alien to the Bible. It was nothing other than the invention of the church many years after Jesus' time on earth. God, to me, was a soloist, not a trio.

So I moved again. From Catholicism through Lutheranism through Calvinism, I emerged as a Unitarian. There was no such designation at the time, but that was the name that was soon attached to those who joined me in this adventurous quest.

The King of Transylvania, a man named John Sigismund, became interested in our movement. In 1568 he invited me to participate in a debate with leaders of the Trinitarian churches. The debate continued for ten days, after which he declared himself an anti-Trinitarian.

Soon thereafter he issued the *Declaration of Torda* which was history's first edict of religious tolerance. He promised freedom and protection to all four of the Christian groups in our land: Catholic, Lutheran, Trinitarian Reformed, and Unitarian. Admittedly, the edict applied only to Christians. It was far short of what you treasure as inclusiveness or pluralism, but it was an historic first step in the unending struggle for tolerance and acceptance.

Under my leadership, and the King's protection, our church flourished and became the most popular and largest in the land.

Meanwhile I continued to evolve in my thinking. I rejected infant baptism. I preached against directing prayers to Jesus. Hardly radical to your way of thinking in the 21st century, I am sure, but dangerously so in the 16th.

Even Socinus, the Italian scholar, who was overseeing the growth of a Unitarian movement in Poland, visited me to attempt to correct my iconoclastic views, but without success. Like good Unitarians should, we parted with an agreement to disagree without being disagreeable. We knew we didn't have to think alike in order to love alike.

Dobre Den. Jmenuji se

CHARLOTTE MASARYK

My roots were in Brooklyn, New York, but my life and my heart belonged to Czechoslovakia.

For forty-four years I was married to, and worked side by side with, Thomas Masaryk, the founding president of that beautiful democratic land.

Together, as a loving and determined team, we carried on a struggle in behalf of human rights, religious tolerance, opposition to anti-Semitism, equality for women, and the establishment of a Czech homeland.

Life began for me in Brooklyn, New York in 1850. I was the daughter of Rudolph Garriague and his wife Charlotte Whiting Garriague. Both of my parents were active members of the First Unitarian Church in Brooklyn. My father had come to this free-thinking faith by way of a Huguenot heritage. Mother boasted often of her earlier correspondence with Ralph Waldo Emerson and her exploration of the possibility of moving to Brook Farm, an experimental cooperative community established by George Ripley and some of his Transcendentalist friends.

My dream was to become a concert pianist. I had sufficient talent that when I was seventeen it was arranged for me to go to Liepzig, Germany to study. An injury to my hand, brought on by excessive practice on the instrument, brought that dream to an end after only three years.

Broken hearted at my ill-fortune, I returned to America, all hope of a musical career lost forever.

I did maintain correspondence with the family with whom I had boarded while in Liepzig and their letters were always full of glowing reports about the young man from Bohemia, named Thomas Masaryk, who had moved into the room I had vacated.

On a return visit to Germany I met this remarkable young man. He was everything they had said, and much, much more. It was magic. We shared so many common interests in books, art, music, politics and religion. We fell in love and married very soon after he completed his doctoral degree at the University of Vienna. First we were married in a civil ceremony at the City Hall in New York, and then a second time with a Unitarian blessing in my parents' home. The wedding was performed by the minister of the Unitarian Church where I had been christened twenty-eight years before.

Life has such a mysterious way of working itself out. I was devastated when my hand was injured and I had to give up the piano. But if I had not suffered that misfortune I would never have moved out of the room that Thomas rented and we would have never met.

Thomas took a position teaching philosophy in the Czech-speaking section of the University of Prague. In a very short period of time he became recognized as a leader in the movement to restore the Czech language and the encouragement of Czech nationalism. I supported him fully in these endeavors and proved my support by learning and becoming fluent in the Czech language.

These were not popular positions in the current political circumstances and he faced increasing opposition from the authorities of the state. His situation become tenuous when he took a strong position in opposition to anti-Semitism in defense of a Jew named Leopold Hilsner, who had been accused of ritual murder. That was an oft-used historical libel used to stir up pogroms against Jews.

28

The outrage on campus and in the city was so great that I feared for my husband's life. In fact, I accompanied him to his lectures at the University, believing that my presence might deter those who wished to assault him. On more than one occasion Thomas found it necessary to bring me back into our house when I was angrily confronting the anti-Semitic student mobs who demonstrated outside.

Thomas soon turned to politics and was elected a member of the Austrian Parliament where he diligently pursued Czech equality, suffrage and autonomy. He did not, at this time, openly advocate independence, but favored the transformation of the Austro-Hungarian Empire into a federation of self-governing provinces.

As he continued his important work, I pursued complimentary missions of my own. I translated into the Czech language John Stuart Mill's treatise on the *Subjection of Women* and wrote a book of my own, *Polygamy and Monogamy*, a strong case for the equality of women.

Thomas supported me in this, as I supported him in his causes. In fact, he became known as a great champion of women's rights. He was wise enough, however, to always give me primary credit and say that he was "only the peddler" of my opinions.

The outbreak of the Great War, which you now call World War I, was a very difficult and trying time for us. My husband and our youngest daughter, Olga, were out of the country at the time hostilities began. But charges of treason were brought against him "in absentia" and he was sentenced to death by the Austro-Hungarian authorities. Thomas joined the Allied Forces in England and spent the war years working for the creation of a Czechoslovakian state. Our other daughter, Alice, was imprisoned. Our elder son, Herbert, died from typhus in a refugee camp, and the younger son, Jan, was drafted into the army. I was not imprisoned, but was subjected to severe persecution and deprivation.

With the end of that horrible war in 1918, the Austro-Hungarian Empire collapsed and the new nation of Czechoslovakia was established. My husband, Thomas Masaryk, was elected its first president. The great dream of his life, which I had come to share, had been fulfilled.

I lived only five more years and thus did not live to see him continue in that leadership position through three succeeding re-elections, until 1935 when old-age forced him to resign in favor of his long-time protégé Eduard Benes.

I dare not close my story without telling you that after World War II, the congregation of the First Unitarian Church in Brooklyn spearheaded a humanitarian relief effort in Czechoslovakia. Out of that effort the Unitarian Service Committee was born.

Dobre Jitro. I am

NORBERT CAPEK

Thank you for inviting me to come here today and tell you my story and share my faith.

I lived such a full and exciting life that I hardly know where to start. At the very beginning I guess would be the appropriate time and place. I was born in the Bohemian town of Radomysil in the year 1870.

At age ten I became an acolyte in the village Catholic Church. I enjoyed participating in the rituals, but got so disillusioned by the cynicism of the priest that I soon quit.

Next I was sent by my family to live with an uncle in Vienna and learn to become a tailor. While there I became acquainted with the non-conformist Baptists. I resigned from the Catholic Church, was baptized by immersion, and became a Bible distributor and traveling evangelist. I founded a number of congregations in the Ukraine and Moravia.

My studies led me to an interest in the history of the Moravian Brethren. These were the followers of Jan Hus who preached a simple faith which emphasized living according to the teachings of Jesus rather than following any creed or dogma. They were, in reality, the original Reformers having arisen a full century before Luther's break with Rome.

I settled for a few years in a Baptist parish in the Saxon town of Plantz, but yearned to return to my native soil and tongue. At the turn of the 20th century there was a growing political movement to establish an autonomous Czech homeland within the Austro-Hungarian Empire and I wished to be a part of that. Simultaneously, my religious thoughts continued to evolve and I was feeling more and more restricted by the Baptist label which I wore.

Thomas Masaryk, a member of Parliament, was the emerging leader of the movement for Czech nationalism. At my request, he granted me an audience to talk about my dreams for a new society which granted complete freedom to any and all religious bodies. At the close of our conversation he said: "You are not a Baptist. You are a Unitarian!" Masaryk had married a woman who had grown up in the First Unitarian Church in Brooklyn, New York. He was also well acquainted with the leaders of American Unitarian Association in Boston.

Both he and his wife, Charlotte, were scheduled to speak at the 1907 Congress on Free Christianity and Religious Progress in Boston. They arranged for me to accompany them to this great gathering. There, for the first time in my life, I met Buddhists, Hindus, Moslems, Sikhs, Taoists, Tibetan followers of the Dalai Lama, Jews, and representatives of every shade of Christianity. I was overwhelmed by the experience.

It was there I first heard the concept of World Patriotism, and the message of One Religion in all religions. One Logos in all the prophets, One Word in all the Churches, One Soul in all the Scriptures, One Father imminent and operant in one Universal Humanity.

At Masaryk's urging I applied for financial assistance from the American Unitarian Association for their help in establishing the Unitarian Church in our homeland. But my appeal fell on deaf ears. The matter was not voted down. It never even came up for discussion. Masaryk said the Association was "like a mother who refuses to nurse her own children." The Unitarians in America, however, more than made up for this slight with a generous outpouring of aid at a later and more critical time.

This may be a good time to share with you a little about another side of my personality: the capricious, playful, fun loving side. I delighted in a good joke or harmless prank. Once when I had been libeled in the public press as the embodiment of Satan, I secretly arranged for a woman to walk down the aisle during one of the Sunday evening sermons, stare for a long time at my feet, then turn to the audience and say, "But he has feet, not hooves!"

Among other things I was a musician. I wrote a number of hymns, some of which are probably in your song books. I was a skillful flutist and organized church orchestras everywhere I went. Once, when invited to preach in a church where I was unknown, the local flutist grew ill and was unable to play. I innocently asked if someone could show me how to hold the instrument and point out where and how I should blow into it. Then I proceeded to play with excellence. The congregation thought it was a miracle!

Another time I was walking down the street as it began to rain. I saw an umbrella in the gutter and picked it up, but it was broken and would not open. I placed it in the nearest trash receptacle, but a young boy came running up behind to return it to me. I then went into a nearby bookstore, deposited the umbrella in a barrel near the door and stood back to watch. A middle-aged woman came to the door, looked out and saw that it was raining, hesitated, looked about, and then lifted it from the barrel and departed. Through the window glass I could see her try to open it and then throw it aside in disgust. A moment later a man lifted it from the sidewalk and it all started all over again. For all I know that umbrella may still be in motion.

But enough of that foolishness. I must hasten on with my story.

Shortly before the outbreak of what is now called World War I, my situation with the Baptists was growing ever more tenuous. My credentials to preach had been revoked and I was threatened with a trial for heresy. Then I was warned by a friendly police official that the Austrian government had placed me on a blacklist and he urged me to leave the country immediately to avoid arrest and imprisonment.

My flight took me, and my family, to a small Slovak Baptist Church on the upper East Side of Manhattan, New York City. A year later we moved across the Hudson and I became minister of the First Slovak Baptist Church in Newark, New Jersey. That congregation grew and prospered under my leadership for the next four years. But when the war was over and the new nation of Czechoslovakia was established I knew I had to return and be a part of the fulfillment of our longtime dream.

In the next few years I not only developed the largest Unitarian congregation in the world, with more than 3,200 members, but also oversaw the development of Unitarianism as a dominant force in the Czechoslovakian nation.

It was a church which reflected my belief that a religion must be first of all for the heart; to bring a cure to the sick heart, bring joy to the sad heart, vigor to the feeble heart, courage to the fearful heart, and put us in harmony with the Infinite.

It was a church that preached and lived a social gospel. We declared that the world was a huge storehouse stuffed with bread, and it was contrary to everything Jesus taught that so many people had to fight so hard simply to stay alive.

It was a church where we established the Flower Communion which is now a regular practice in so many congregations around the world. Everyone brings a flower and everyone leaves with a flower, not knowing from whom it has come. The unbroken web of our humanity and the circle of nature and its cycles which never end.

Then, in 1939, the Nazis came. The American Unitarians pleaded with me to leave Prague and come to New York. They promised positions to both me and my son-in-law, who served as my associate pastor. But I could not accept that generous offer. My place was with my people in their time of trouble.

In 1941, I, along with my daughter Zora, was arrested by the Gestapo and charged with treason for having listened to radio reports from the British Broadcasting Company. A court found me innocent and recommended that the two years I had already spent in prison be my sentence. But as soon as I was released the Gestapo arrested me again and deported me to Dachau. In October 1942 I was transferred to Hartheim Castle, near Linz, Austria, where I was put to death in a gas chamber.

But do not allow this somber ending to depress you. My life was a vibrant one, full of happiness and joy. My most memorable book was entitled *Toward a Sunnier Shore*. That is the way I want you to remember me.

Good Morning. I am

BELA BARTOK

I was a Unitarian, but had my own personal Trinity. If I had ever crossed myself it would have been "in the name of Nature, Art and Science." Those, to me, were the true essentials of life.

They are real. All else is speculative and hypothetical. Why do people demand to have answers to unanswerable questions? Why do we expend so much time and energy fighting over different interpretations of the creation of the universe? Why not just admit that we cannot know that which is unknowable and go on enjoying the beauty and grandeur of life all around us?

I never had much patience with religious speculation and all the tortured word manipulations of the theologians. To me it was just so much mumbo-jumbo. But I never blamed Jesus for that. He was a great moralist, who taught many valuable lessons. But he was not the mythical character his later followers tried to make him out to be.

So, that, in essence, is my Credo. It is where I ended up, but not, of course, where I began.

I was born in 1881 in Hungary, which was then a part of the Austro-Hungarian Empire. My father died when I was very young and my mother took our family to Bratislava in her native Slovakia. That is where I grew up.

Mother was an accomplished pianist and there is little doubt that I inherited my musical abilities from her. Due to a childhood illness brought on by an inoculation for smallpox, I spent much of my first five years indoors listening as she played. By the age of nine I was composing music of my own.

I was fortunate in being able to study at the great Academy of Music in Budapest. After graduation I pursued a career as a concert pianist and composer, and accepted a position as instructor at the academy.

While still a young man I developed an interest in folk music and the traditions which brought it into being. I set out in earnest to learn all I could about the music and culture of Slovakia, Hungary, Romania, Serbia, even down into Algeria in North Africa. I became obsessed with this study and determined to spend my life collecting and categorizing this treasure trove.

What I was striving to do was to identify both the distinct and the unifying elements in the music of the people which transcended all lines of nationality while retaining a uniqueness all its own. You would probably call this "multiculturalism" today.

When World War I engulfed Europe it was called "unpatriotic." The old Empire dissolved and ethnic identities and loyalties became intense. I was accused of disloyalty for maintaining an interest in the music of people who were now the enemies of Hungary. Oh, how I yearned for a sense of universalism which was not bound by artificial boundaries of race or clan!

But I am supposed to be telling you how I became a Unitarian. Let me step back and start again. My early training was Roman Catholic, but long before I reached maturity I had turned my back on the church and was an atheist. I found it incomprehensible that people claimed that "God created man in His own image" when it was obvious that "man had created God in his own image." Living without a faith in God posed no problems for me. I was quite happy in my state of disbelief.

Then, in 1907, I traveled to Transylvania to study the culture and music of a sub-group called Szekely which had maintained a degree of isolation from the rest of Hungary and preserved many ancient customs. It was while in Transylvania that I discovered

Unitarianism. Transylvania, of course, as you know, was the birthplace of our rational faith four centuries earlier.

The Unitarian approach to life made sense to me. It spoke to my condition. It met my deepest needs. When my son, Bela Jr. was born in 1910, I announced my conversion to Unitarianism and our family associated itself with the Mission House Congregation in Budapest.

My decision to formally announce my conversion at that time was deliberate and a gift to my newborn son. By declaring myself a Unitarian I made it possible for my son to avoid mandatory Catholic education as declared by the state.

All the while I continued composing and gained increasing recognition as the leading Hungarian composer of the 20th century. I realize that sounds boastful of me, but I am only reporting to you what others have said about me.

In the years between the two horrible World Wars I walked a tightrope, continuing my musical career while opposing the rise of Fascism and Nazism all around me. For a period I was suspended from teaching at the Academy for political reasons. I forbade my music to be performed or broadcast in Mussolini's Italy and Hitler's Germany. As the political situation worsened I reluctantly decided that I must get away. I shipped all my papers and musical scores to America and soon followed with my wife.

While living in New York I became ill with leukemia and was supported by ASCAP, the American Society for Composers, Authors, and Publishers. I fought to stay alive so that I would be able to return from exile to my native land. But it was not to be.

Less that six months after the end of the war in Europe I died and was buried at Woodlawn Cemetery in New York with the minister of All Souls Unitarian Church officiating.

In 1988, as the Iron Curtain lifted, my son Bela Jr., then president of the Hungarian Unitarian Church, arranged for reburial in Budapest and the erection of a statue of me in front of our old church in that ancient city which I loved.

Greetings to you! I am

THOMAS AIKENHEAD

I do not know exactly why I have been invited to speak to you today. I wrote no books. I founded no movements. All I am remembered for is for being hanged as a heretic.

If that qualifies me to share a Credo with you, then I am delighted to have been asked.

I was born in Edinburgh, Scotland in the year 1676. My father was a surgeon and pharmacist. But I remember little of either my father or mother since they both died when I was quite young and I was left an orphan.

At age 17 I was admitted to Edinburgh University and was transformed by what I found in the library of that distinguished institution. I discovered the works of philosophers such as Spinoza, Hobbes, and Descartes. These were men whom I had heard maligned and vilified, but knew little of what they believed. But as I took advantage of the opportunity to read what they had actually written, rather than accepting what their opponents said that they had said, I found myself exhilarated by their willingness to fearlessly explore great ideas and apply reason in the search of answers.

I read Miguel Servetus' *The Restoration of Christianity* with special interest. He enunciated so clearly and convincingly many ideas with which I had been wrestling, but had not yet been able to clarify for myself.

Fortunately I became acquainted with these great thinkers when I did, for in 1697, while I was still a student, the Scottish authorities condemned all these men as "atheistical, erroneous, or profane and vicious" and removed them from the shelves of all libraries and bookstores.

I was found guilty as charged and sentenced to be hanged. When I pleaded with the judges for leniency they agreed to a lighter sentence if the Church of Scotland petitioned them in my behalf.

Rather than doing so, the General Assembly of the Church, meeting in Edinburgh, asked for my immediate execution as an example to others that "impiety and profanity" would not be tolerated in the land.

So, on January 8, 1697, I went to the gallows. I was only 21 years of age at that time.

But the significance of my death may be that I was the last person to be executed for blasphemy in any of the British Isles.

A hearty Good Morning to you. I am

JOHN BIDDLE

I have been called the "Father of English Unitarianism." Whether that is a deserved appellation is not mine to say.

In the intervening years between the publication in English of Socinus' *Rakovian Cathechism* and my earliest pronouncements on the subject of the Trinity there had been a number of Church of England clergymen who had, at least, carried on a flirtation with that supposed heresy.   In addition, quite a number of Anabaptists had emigrated from the Continent bringing with them a variation of Arianism.

Nor was I the person who organized the first Unitarian congregation. That honor belongs to Theophilus Lindsey nearly a century later. You will have to wait to hear his story later when he shares it with you in his own words.

As for me, I was born in Wotton-under-Edge in Gloucestershire in the year 1615. I was educated at Magdalen College at Oxford. After graduation I returned to my native Gloucestershire where I was appointed Headmaster of the free school.

I was a schoolteacher and a lay theologian. I was not a member of the clergy, but I dare say I knew the Holy Scriptures better than most of them. In fact, by the time I had achieved maturity I had committed the entire New Testament to memory.

Even before I laid eyes on the writing of Socinus I had independently reached the conclusion that the doctrine of the Trinity and the elevation of Jesus to a position as Second Person in the Godhead, co-equal with the Father, was clearly without Scriptural validity.

My lively interest in theological matters led me to convene frequent discussions with my academic colleagues on a variety of these concerns.

Just before my 30th birthday I wrote, but did not publish, a treatise entitled *Twelve Arguments Drawn from Scripture Wherein Commonly Received Opinion Touching the Deity of the Holy Spirit Is Clearly and Fully Refuted.* This paper was intended only for discussion with my fellow teachers and nothing more. I had no intention of publishing it for public distribution.

But one of my fellows, who was envious of my position as Headmaster and desired it for himself, gave a copy to the authorities of the Church. As a result I was called before a Parliamentary Committee and convicted under a law known as the Draconian Act, which said that "any person willingly by preaching, teaching, printing or writing maintains that the Father is not God, the Son is not God, or that the Holy Ghost is not God, or that the three are not one eternal God, or that Christ is not God equal with the Father shall be adjudged guilty . . . and shall suffer the penalty of death without benefit of clergy."

I was found guilty, but my judges decreed leniency and I was spared execution. Rather they sentenced me to prison for an unspecified length of time. Three years later I was released on bail.

While I was imprisoned I had more that enough time for quiet thought. I decided that if they thought the issues which I had raised were of sufficient importance to use such extreme measures to silence me, those issues were important enough for me to publicly pursue.

So as soon as I was released I proceeded at once to publish the paper that had gotten me into trouble in the first place. I was immediately re-arrested. My tract was burned, and I was sent back to my cell.

I set about feverishly writing more and smuggling those writings out of the prison. Subsequent pamphlets continued to elevate God the Father as the only deity and subordinate both the Son and the Holy Spirit.

Influential friends intervened in my behalf and I was released from Staffordshire prison and placed under what amounted to house arrest. That arrangement lasted for little more than a year when I was once again, for the third time, returned to my dungeon.

In 1652 Cromwell rose to the position of Lord Protector of England. He certainly was not in agreement with my theological positions. But as much as he despised my doctrines he hated the Church of England even more. This was a classic case of "he who is the enemy of my enemy is my friend." Regardless of motivation, Cromwell arranged for my release.

This time I used my freedom to gather a relatively small group of like-minded persons for Sunday worship and discussion. Sometimes we were called Unitarians, but more frequently referred to as Biddlellians.

Later that same year I published the *Two-Fold Catechism*, which was essentially an updating of Socinian teachings.

This was more than the establishment could tolerate. Once again I was arrested and convicted. But this time I was sentenced to death. And again, Cromwell stepped forward as my protector. He was reluctant to having me executed and, instead, arranged for me to be exiled to the Scilly Isles.

They are an archipelago off the southwest coast of Land's End. He also granted me a subsidy of 100 crowns per year to cover basic living expenses.

Six years later Cromwell was overthrown and the monarchy

restored. During the ensuing period of turmoil I returned from exile and rejoined my friends. We reestablished our secret meetings for worship. But in 1662 my house was raided during one of our services. I was convicted of preaching a heretical doctrine. This time I was only fined for my transgression.

However, I did not have the required 100 pounds to pay the fine and for the sixth, and final, time I was taken away to prison. There I died in a matter of months.

Mine is hardly a tale of success and triumph as the world usually judges such matters. But it is a true account of how the rational faith of Unitarianism was introduced to England, and that is glory enough for me.

Good Morning. I am

JOSEPH PRIESTLEY

I was trained for the Presbyterian ministry in my native England in the middle years of the 18th century. A product of the Enlightenment I had broad interests in philosophy, theology, and science.

In my early years, in addition to serving as minister of a series of rural and small-town dissenting congregations, I also worked as a schoolteacher, a librarian, a writer, and a literary tutor to an Earl.

When I was 40 years of age I settled at the New Meeting Birmingham, which was reputed to be the most liberal church in all of England. It was there I gained my reputation as a theological troublemaker to some and as a prophetic leader to others.

Prior to this time Unitarianism was either Arian, which taught that Jesus was divine, but not equal to God, or Socinian, which taught that Christ was not divine but was worthy of being invoked in worship.

As a student of Scripture I said that the early Church was Unitarian in regard to God, but humanitarian in regard to Jesus. I was a scientist, and an avowed materialist. I believed that everything was material, that is, physical. I rejected the idea of the spirit or soul. Thus, I could accept the idea of a physical resurrection, but not the existence of a soul.

Shortly after moving to Birmingham I was invited to join a group of the city's intellectual leaders, including Josiah Wedgwood the pottery maker and the philosopher Erasmus Darwin who developed the theory of evolution for which his grandson, Charles, later provided physical evidence. We called ourselves the Lunar Society because we met on the Monday nearest the full moon each month. That way we had light to guide us home when our sessions were over. Others called us The Lunatics.

The New Meeting had an associate minister who did most of the weekday work of the congregation. I preached and taught on Sundays, but was free on other days to pursue my scientific experiments.

One of my scientific discoveries came about in a most unusual manner. Our manse was situated right next to a brewery and its noxious fumes disturbed my wife greatly. I decided to study the matter to see if there was anything I could find. I did not find a way to diminish the brewery fumes, but I did discover oxygen.

Another of my finds was carbonation. So whenever you enjoy a carbonated soft drink, think of me.

On the trips to London to meet with scientific societies I had the opportunity to become acquainted with both Benjamin Franklin and Thomas Jefferson. We shared many common interests, both religious and political.

When the French Revolution broke out in 1790 I spoke out strongly in favor of it; just as I had done regarding the American Revolution a few years before. Needless to say this aroused considerable reaction from conservative churchmen and royalists.

The following year, in celebration of Bastille Day, a celebratory dinner was held by supporters of the Revolution at a Birmingham hotel. Leaders of the Anglican High Church party organized a mob to march on the hotel, but they arrived after the dinner was over and most of the celebrants had left for home. The mob then turned their attention to the New Meeting House, which they burned to the ground. Next they burned our home and my laboratory, destroying my lifetime of books and papers.

Our family was able to escape unharmed. Unharmed physically, that is. My wife never recovered from the emotional trauma of that terrifying experience.

The rioting continued for three days before it was put down by the police. The authorities did not intervene until the arsonists had done all they wanted to do. The Anglican priest who was their leader was shortly thereafter rewarded by being made a Bishop of the Church.

I moved to another congregation in Hackney, but after three years my wife and I decided it would be best for us to emigrate to America, where our two sons had preceded us.

We settled in Philadelphia where I reestablished my friendship with Thomas Jefferson. Franklin had died in the intervening years. I also became friends with George Washington, John Adams, and the Universalist physician Benjamin Rush.

I also organized the first congregation in America to wear the name Unitarian. After my wife died I then moved on to a frontier town on the Susquehanna River where I established another Unitarian chapel and continued preaching until my death in 1804.

Even though I founded the first congregation to be called Unitarian in the New World, it would be a mistake to think that I began the movement on those shores. Anti-Trinitarian and anti-Calvinist ideas were rising like yeast all over New England at that same time. It was only a matter of approximately two decades before William Ellery Channing had led hundreds of Congregationalist Churches into the Unitarian fold.

But my influence on them was negligible at best. In fact, many in New England went to great lengths to disassociate themselves from my views.

Isn't that a Unitarian thing to do?

Good Morning. I am

JOSIAH WEDGWOOD

My birth in 1730 was the occasion for considerable interest in the village of Burslam, England. I was the thirteenth, and final, child of the potter Thomas Wedgwood and his wife. There were six boys and six girls. My arrival, I am told, stimulated more than a little wagering at the local pub as to how the tie would be broken.

Before I reached my ninth birthday I had left school and begun my apprenticeship in the family trade at Churchyard Works.

Two years later I was stricken with smallpox, which left me with a severely crippled leg that made it impossible for me to work at the potter's wheel. I then turned to experimentation with glazes and the study of methods to make pottery production more efficient. Since these were the two things that later brought me fame and fortune, you might say my disability was a blessing in disguise.

That is the way I tried to look at it. My philosophy was that one should seek to improve those things that could be improved, and to accept in good spirits those things that could not. Even when my leg had to be amputated, three decades later, I designated the anniversary of my radical surgery as St. Amputation's Day and hosted an annual picnic for my workers.

My experiments with glazes resulted in the creation of cream-coloured vessels which captured the fancy of Queen Charlotte, wife of George III. Her acquisitions permitted me to be designated as Potter to the Queen, and this particular style to be known as Queen's Ware. After this I began to receive orders from all over Europe and the far reaches of the Empire.

By this time I had entered into a partnership with Thomas

Bentley. What began as a business arrangement became a friendship that lasted a lifetime.

Having outgrown our local facilities, we moved to Liverpool and built a new factory call Etruria. At that time I commissioned the construction of an entire village to provide housing for my employees. That was an unprecedented thing to do.

At the Etruria factory I instituted a new system of pottery production. Up to that time each individual worker was responsible for a particular piece of work from start to finish. I subdivided the task into the categories of mixing, shaping, firing and glazing and allocated each job to a specialist. That became known as "the division of labor" which ushered England into the Industrial Age.

I was privileged to live in a great era of human history. The dawn of the new age demanded that workmen begin to perceive time not as a cyclical event that rolls the seasons around in predictable sequence, but as something finite, valuable, and controllable.

The farmer, shepherds, and fishermen who were migrating into the cities in search of employment needed to learn the importance of regular and punctual attention to their jobs. I chose to use one of their favorite pastimes as an instrument of that lesson.

Kicking a ball around—football, or soccer if you prefer—was without rules or time restraints. Sometimes it was a competition of kicking the ball from one village to another. It was not unusual for that to take all day, or even several days.

I took leadership in codifying the rules of the game and establishing a ninety minute time period in which it had to be concluded. In that way they learned that time was important and a task had to be completed within specified limits. Had you ever considered that to have been an innovation of the Industrial Age?

I was privileged to be associated with a remarkable group who met monthly under the name of the Lunar Society. Among its members were such renowned figures as the philosopher Erasmus Darwin, the minister/scientist Joseph Priestley, and steam engine inventer James Watt.

Erasmus Darwin joined Bentley as one of my closest friends. In fact, even our families became intertwined. My daughter Susanna married his son Robert, and in the following generation my granddaughter Emma was the wife of his grandson, the famous naturalist Charles Darwin.

Since this is supposed to be my Credo, I should tell you something about my religious heritage. Our family had been Quakers, but when my sister Catherine married the dissenting minister Rev. William Willett we associated ourselves with his church, which later became Unitarian. My Unitarian views were greatly strengthened through association with Priestley.

As unorthodox as my dissenting, or Unitarian, beliefs might have been, they were not nearly as liberal as those of my partner Thomas Bentley. He had a long involvement with the Octagon Chapel which sought an inclusive creed which would include all religions.

He later built a chapel in London where morality was taught rather than any creed. He believed that all were children of one benevolent parent. He often asked, rhetorically, "Do not Jews and Gentiles, Christians and Mohamentans, own his power, his wisdom, his goodness?"

He urged me to join him in building the chapel in London, and I did make a financial contribution. But at that time I was more concerned with finding a suitable replacement for the aging Rev. Willett at our Unitarian Chapel in Newcastle.

It is ironic, is it not, that what Bentley was putting forward in the late 18th century is what Unitarian Universalism has become in the 21st. Yet, at the time, he and Priestley engaged in frequent spirited conversations which left Priestley frustrated because he could not convince Bentley to become a Christian.

My concerns for social justice were of long-standing. Much earlier I had worked with the Quakers to establish the Society for the Abolition of the Slave Trade. You may be familiar with that organization's seal which I designed and distributed widely. It was the image of a black slave, kneeling with arms reaching upward in supplication. Surrounding the figure were the words: AM I NOT A MAN AND A BROTHER?

I would prefer to be remembered as the creator of that seal and sentiment more than for anything else I ever made or did.

Good Morning. I am

THEOPHILUS LINDSEY

I was the founder of the first Unitarian church in England in 1774 after resigning from the Anglican ministry.

Let me explain how that came about. I was born, the youngest son of a Scotch businessman, in Middlewich, Cheshire in 1723. Through the generosity of a group of women in our town I was able to attend Cambridge, where I graduated with honors. Leaders of the University urged me to accept a faculty position and spend my life as an academic.

I chose, instead, to pursue further theological studies and was ordained a minister in the Church of England. My first assignment was as private chaplain to a nobleman. I spent the next few years in frequent travel about the Continent in his spiritual service.

Next I became minister of a small parish in Yorkshire. It was while there I formed a close friendship with Rev. Francis Blackburne, the archdeacon of Cleveland whose step-daughter became my wife.

From there I moved to a parish in Dorsetshire for seven years. During this period my intense study of the Scriptures led to serious doubts about the Trinity and many other doctrines of the Church. So strong were my feelings on these matters that I was sorely tempted to resign from the ministry.

I knew I was not alone in my skepticism on doctrinal matters. Many of my fellow clergymen shared my feelings. I rationalized that if they stayed in the church despite their doubts, there was no reason I could not do the same. I convinced myself, for the time being, that it was best to stay and work for change from within the institution.

Primarily through my father-in-law's influence I was offered a parish in Ireland which would have inevitably led to an appointment as a bishop. I turned it down and chose, instead, to resettle in the parish of Catterick in Yorkshire. This was a parish of poor and working class people. I threw myself into the work with such unbridled enthusiasm that many accused me of having become a Methodist!

The church organized efforts to provide food, medicine, nursing, books, and other social services to the poor. I felt it was imperative to provide practical expressions of Christian compassion in addition to words of comfort and hope.

In 1763 my wife and I organized the first Sunday School for religious instruction.

While being quite happy in my parish work, I remained troubled by the theological positions I appeared to espouse while deep in my mind and heart I knew I had long since rejected them.

I spent several days in the home of my father-in-law, Archdeacon Blackburne and two non-subscribing Presbyterians whom he had invited in for conversation. One of these men was Dr. Joseph Priestley, who was already referring to himself as a Unitarian. I confessed my confusions to Priestley and sought his counsel. He advised me to stay in the Church as long as it was possible for me to do so.

Shortly after this Blackburne and a group of his friends convened a meeting at Feather's Tavern where they drew up a petition to Parliament asking that clergymen of the church be relieved from the burden of subscribing to the 39 articles of faith and be "restored to their undoubted rights as Protestants of interpreting Scripture for themselves." Two hundred and fifty signatures were obtained. The names of several Bishops were included. Many others who believed as we did refused to sign. The renowned theologian William Paley probably spoke for most of them when he said he "could not afford to keep a conscience."

In 1772, the House of Commons refused to even receive the petition. Their negative vote was repeated the following year.

I knew I could hesitate no longer. I prepared for publication an *Apology for Resigning the Vicarage of Catterick* and delivered a tender farewell sermon to my beloved congregation. Then, like Abraham of old, I "went out, knowing not whither."

I was fifty years of age, of frail health, and totally without funds. Those whom I had considered my dearest friends turned against me. Other Feather's Tavern petitioners condemned me, saying that my actions had injured their cause. Francis Blackburne refused to speak to me for many years. Others in his family offered my wife a considerable sum of money, which would have supported her in luxury for the rest of her life, if she would leave me. She refused their generous offer.

It seemed to me that there must be many who loved the Church of England and the beauty of its worship while disagreeing with its dogma. I decided I would try to gather them together. We moved to London and rented two small furnished rooms and I set to work on a liberal revision of the Book of Common Prayer.

Dr. Priestley rallied behind me. He convinced a few influential friends to rent an empty auction house on Essex Street. It was there, on April 17, 1774 that we held the first meeting of the Unitarian Chapel. About 200 people were in attendance at that original service. Priestley himself attended, as did his friend Dr. Benjamin Franklin who was in England representing the American colonies. Franklin donated five guineas to our building fund and was in regular attendance at our meetings as long as he remained in London.

The congregation attracted a number of persons of prominence including scientists, nobility and members of Parliament. Within two years we were able to move into more spacious and suitable quarters in Kensington. The hall on Essex Street has remained headquarters for British Unitarianism to this very day.

In 1783 I wrote a review of Unitarian history, showing it had ancient roots in Christianity and was not a new or insignificant sect.

When Dr. Priestley came under violent attack I rose to his defense.

At age 70 I resigned and never set foot inside our Chapel again. My heart and soul were there, but I felt it better for my successors to physically remove myself from the premises.

I mentioned earlier that I was in feeble health at age 50. The Unitarian adventure surely restored me both spiritually and physically. I lived to the age of 85 and died knowing that my views had spread widely throughout the British Isles and France and that King's Chapel in Boston had adopted my revised version of the Book of Common Prayer.

Good Morning. I am

ANNA LETITIA AIKEN BARBAULD

I was a poet, an educator, a political activist, and the wife of a Unitarian minister.

My father was also a minister of the Dissenting Presbyterians. They were those who had withdrawn from the Presbyterians by refusing to ascribe to the Trinitarian clause of the Westminster Confession. You might call them pre-Unitarians.

I was born in 1743 in Leicestershire where my father taught at the Warrington Academy. This was a school for Dissenters. Colleges in England at that time were not open to those who were not members of the established Church.

Joseph Priestley, the famed Unitarian preacher and scientist also taught at Warrington. It was he who inspired me when I was quite young to write poetry. In fact, one of my earliest published poems was a rather whimsical verse on the Furniture in Priestley's Study.

When I reached maturity I married a Unitarian minister named Rochemont Barbauld. His grandparents had been Huguenot refugees from France. We were settled with a congregation in Suffolk. The marriage was a very happy one, and many of my early poems celebrated the thousand pleasant arts we shared together.

But before I tell you more about myself, I should relate to you some of my thoughts about religion. After all, you did invite me here to present my Credo.

Where should I begin? First, I suppose, by saying that I had some precise ideas about church architecture. I always despised those family pews. I called them gloomy little solitary cells, planned by the spirit of aristocracy. I recommended instead that chapels should be built in the form of amphitheatres where the minister could be easily seen by everyone present.

Also, I frequently said, in my day, that the people should have a much greater share in the performance of the service. There should be lots of singing by the congregation. Anything to make those Sabbath hours more agreeable for all. Both my minister father, and my minister husband thought I was a bit too outspoken on this matter.

But I wanted a religion with joy. Too much of what went on in most churches only added to the gathering of gloom. What most churches taught could do nothing other than contribute to the sense of despair. No one who embraced the idea of a future of eternal torment, pre-determined by a God of wrath, could be any-thing other than gloomy. What a strange absurdity to believe that sins committed against an Infinite Being were deserving of infinite punishment. No one could have such ideas often in his thoughts and still be cheerful.

In this life we honor moral character, and virtuous and charitable behavior. Why, then, should we embrace a religion which teaches that the Creator is oblivious to that which we cherish? When a good man draws near the end of his life, not free from all faults, but pure from crime; a life well-spent in the habitual exercise of those virtues which adorn and dignify human nature, he ought to do so with a reliance on the justice of God rather than in vain pleading for His mercy. Why do people worship a Creator whom they believe is less just and less loving than those He has created?

As for me, I passionately reject the heart-withering perspectives of never-ending punishment and am prepared to throw myself into the arms of Eternal Love.

So you see, I was both a Unitarian and a Universalist more than two centuries before the two groups decided to get together.

Now, let me get back to the chronology of my life. In addition to our Unitarian Chapel, my husband and I organized a boarding school. I attempted a number of innovations in education. Foremost among them, perhaps, was the idea of getting the students away from the classroom to visit Parliament, the Courts, places of business, and the homes of famous people who lived in our vicinity. Perhaps it was I who invented field-trips!

Rochemont and I were unable to produce a child of our own, but my brother and sister-in-law agreed to conceive and give birth to a son who was given to us for adoption in his earliest infancy. In this wonderful new phase of my life my poetry turned to children and the ways in which they learned to appreciate the beauty of nature. My book *Hymns in Prose for Children* emphasized the use of nature as an expression of the love of God.

The next decade of my life was focused on political and social concerns. I supported Wilberforce in his struggle to eliminate slavery. I defended Priestley against charges of heresy. I challenged the 1792 Proclamation Against Seditious Writings by publishing the book *Sins of Government, Sins of the Nation*, to protest our declaration of war against France.

Tragedy came into our lives around the turn of the century. My beloved husband, Rochemont, developed what would now be recognized as a mental illness. He had frequent fits of violence. On several occasions my life was placed in jeopardy. Friends implored me to have him placed in an asylum, but I could not bring myself to do so. Rather, I hired guards to watch over him while we remained at our home.

But one spring day in 1808 he escaped from his guard and drowned himself in a nearby river. I valiantly struggled to carry on, but my life was never quite the same for the seventeen years I survived.

But please do not think that I grew gloomy or sad. My faith
would never have permitted that. Among the last poems I wrote
was this:

> Life! We've been long together,
> Through pleasant and through cloudy weather,
> 'Tis hard to part when friends are dear,—
> Perhaps 'twill cost a sigh, a tear,
> Then steal away, give little warning,
> Choose thine own time.
> Say not "Goodnight," but in some brighter clime
> Bid me "Good morning."

Good Morning. I am

MARY WOLLSTONECRAFT

I have been called the inspiration of the 19th and 20th century women's liberation movements. I hope that continues into your 21st century as well.

Though I am primarily remembered for my advocacy of the rights of women, I prefer to think of myself as one who fought for all those who were suppressed and disenfranchised by the imposition of false and debilitating stereotypes.

I often said I did not wish women to have power over men, but only to be permitted to have power over themselves.

I spoke forcefully against society placing a higher premium on property rights than it did on human rights.

I openly advocated breaking up the large estates in England and distributing the land to the farmers who tilled the fields.

If a radical is one who strives to transform the roots of a culture, then I am proud to be identified as one.

It would be nice to say that these beliefs derived from my affiliation with the Unitarian Church. It would be more reasonable, however, to say that I chose Unitarianism because it alone, among the religious teachings and practices of my era, reflected the rational approach and humanitarian ideals which I had discovered and claimed for myself.

How I came to those ideas I cannot say. Certainly my childhood was not so different from that of other English girls of that time. Did I neglect to tell you that I was born in 1759? My father was a weaver who frequently physically abused my mother during drunken rages. I never completely recovered emotionally from the memories of those attacks.

I was largely self-educated, and from my teenage years supported myself through a series of jobs of the kind which were open to women: Seamstress, Governess, Schoolteacher.

In my early 20's, I was introduced to a circle of intellectual friends of my Unitarian minister, Richard Price. He periodically convened discussion groups of persons such as Thomas Paine, William Blake, Joseph Priestley, William Wordsworth, and William Godwin. Remember this final name. I will return to him later. Rev. Price often involved me in these scholarly discussions. As a result I found a position as translator and editor of *The Analytical Review* which distributed Unitarian writings.

When the French Revolution broke out in 1789, Reverend Price preached a sermon supporting the rebels. Edmund Burke responded with a strong denunciation of Price for his position. I, then, rose to the challenge and wrote *A Vindication of the Rights of Men*, which praised those who fought for the rights of the common people against the privileges of aristocracy.

Thomas Paine also responded to Burke with his *Rights of Man*, and received much more attention for his work than I had for mine. Both of us, however were accused of threatening the monarchy. The threat of retaliation was so serious that Paine found it necessary to emigrate to France, just as he had moved to the American Colonies during their uprising a decade earlier.

My next writing, a major work, was entitled *A Vindication of the Rights of Women*. This subject had been churning in my mind ever since I had read Rousseau's *Emile*, in which he proposed a different kind of education for girls than that given boys. He wanted girls to be educated in the domestic arts only, and taught to be submissive to men in all things.

To the contrary, I said, if a woman is not prepared by education to become the companion of man, she will stop the progress of knowledge, for truth must be common to all, or it will be inefficacious with respect to its influence on general practice.

To those who expressed the concern that if women were educated they would cease to be good wives, I answered: "Make women rational creatures, and free citizens, and they will quickly become good wives—that is if men do not neglect their duties of husbands and fathers."

I never hesitated to point out the guilt of both Judaism and Christianity in denigrating the position of women. It seemed to me abundantly clear that if God was just, as it was claimed, then He would not have created one sex as superior to the other.

Another point at which I took issue with orthodox religion was the idea of original sin. This concept, to me, was worse than a farce. To believe and teach that all humans were inherently evil was nothing other than a cruel trick by the prelates and theologians to hold people hostage to the church. I believed in the human potential for unlimited growth when all people, men and women, were set free to become their true selves.

Oh yes, I said I would get back to William Godwin. That is exactly what I did. I moved to France in 1792 to write a book about the French Revolution. While there I entered into a common-law marriage with an American named Gilbert Imlay. I became pregnant; gave birth to a daughter; and was deserted by the father. This was followed by a period of depression during which I made at least two attempts at suicide.

I thought much about mortality and immortality at this time. I concluded that I could not imagine the possibility that I should cease to exist, or that my active, restless spirit, equally alive to joy and deep sorrow, should be only organized dust . . . ready to spring abroad the moment the spring snaps or the spark goes out.

Surely something resides in this heart that is not perishable—and life is more than a dream.

Thoughts like that, I believe, brought me out of my depression and returned me to England. There I reestablished my friendship with William Godwin. Our friendship deepened and we were married. Two years later I died of puerperal fever 10 days after the birth of my daughter Mary.

So, my Credo ends. But there are three additional comments I want to make.

First, I want you to be aware that Mary grew up to marry the poet Percy Blythe Shelley and to be the author of *Frankenstein*.

Secondly, I want you to know that I take great pride in the fact that Susan B. Anthony and Elizabeth Cady Stanton dedicated their *History of Women's Suffrage* to me.

And lastly, I want you to know that I always acted on principle.

Good Morning. I am

ROBERT ASPLAND

John Biddle brought Unitarian thinking to England, and Theophilus Lindsey and his wife established the first Unitarian Church on Essex Street in London. Neither was I an influential preacher of Unitarian doctrines to compare with others such as Joseph Priestley.

But, I do believe I am justly credited with creating the institutional structures which brought coherence and stability to the movement. I take great satisfaction in being remembered as the "Father of Organized Unitarianism in Great Britain."

There was never any doubt in my mind while I was growing up that I would become a minister. Father was a shopkeeper in Wicken, Cambridgeshire where we regularly attended the Baptist Church.

I remember, as a very young lad, taking copious notes of sermons which impressed me, and carefully filing them away for future use for when I would become a preacher.

My only period of doubt came near the end of my ministerial training at the University of Aberdeen as I grew increasingly uncomfortable with some of the Baptist teachings. I withdrew from school and took secular employment while trying to think through the direction of my future.

Fortunately for me, I came under the influence of John Evans, minister of a Baptist Chapel in London who, like myself, was moving away from Calvinistic thinking in the direction of Unitarian beliefs. He arranged for me to be appointed minister to a congregation on the Isle of Wight which was receptive to my liberal ideas. The year was 1801 and I was barely nineteen at the time.

Five years later I became minister of one of the most influential Unitarian congregations in the country. That was the New Gravel Pit Chapel in Hackney where Priestley had served before leaving England for residence in the United States. The chapel was nominally Presbyterian, but had a series of Unitarian leaders prior to my arrival.

From that settled base I enthusiastically set myself to the task of bringing organization to the loose-knit fellowship of Unitarian congregations throughout the British Isles.

Arrangements were made with Richard Wright, a General Baptist minister, to leave his settlement and become a missionary for spreading Unitarianism. The General Baptists were an off-shoot of the Anabaptists who believed that salvation was for all, and not just the "elect," as taught by Calvin. Wright came to his Unitarianism through Universalism, having evolved in his theology to believe that a loving God would freely give salvation to all of His creation.

During twelve years of criss-crossing the British Isles, traveling as much as 3,000 miles a year, often on foot, Wright preached and organized in as many as five hundred locations. The number of Unitarian congregations grew from around 20 to nearly 250 in England, Scotland, Wales and Ireland. The credit, of course, belongs to Richard Wright, but I take great satisfaction in having organized the Society which set him forth and supported him in this monumental work.

At the same time, I started and published two journals to further the cause of liberal religious thought. *The Monthly Repository*, begun in 1806 was highly influential as an instrument of unifying the scattered congregations into a coherent structure. Then in 1815 I started publication of *The Christian Reformer*, which was not as scholarly in nature and designed to speak more directly to the less educated working class.

In addition, I was active in efforts to move the government in the direction of tolerance. In 1819 I organized the *Association for the Protection of the Civil Rights of Unitarians*. But I did not limit my concerns to such a narrow constituency. I worked diligently with other Protestant Dissenters and Catholics to achieve civil liberties for all.

Almost from the beginning of my public career I had close and cooperative relationships with Jews. Many attended services at the Chapel where I preached. But I always made it clear that I had no interest in converting them to Christianity, my brand or any other. Rather, I felt we had much to learn from one another and we should interact with mutual respect and admiration.

Another civic issue which demanded my attention was the way prisoners were treated in our jails. I considered it barbaric and antithetical to civilization. I often said, "Our penal laws are written in blood."

Likewise I took strong positions from my pulpit in opposition to war and the culture of violence created by nationalism. I pleaded for a movement to break the never-ending cycles of aggression and retaliation, which always led to counter-retaliation and more acts of revenge. Followers of the Prince of Peace should have none of that!

When my English predecessor, Joseph Priestley, came under attack in America for his too-scientific and too-materialistic theology, I rose to his defense. In particular, I felt the great American leader, William Ellery Channing, was much too harsh in his criticism and I did not hesitate to say so.

In fact, that may be a valid summary of my life. Many of my peers said of me: "He never hesitated to say so! On a wide variety of issues. Even when silence would have been a greater virtue!" Many thought I was overly aggressive in pursuing goals I thought were important. They said I was less patient than I should have been with those who wished to make progress at a more leisurely pace. Perhaps that is true.

But when I died in 1845 and was laid to rest beside the Chapel I had served for forty years, I looked back with very few regrets and with a great pride in the Unitarian organization in my country, which had come into being under my leadership and persistent prodding.

Buenos Dias. I am

JOSE MARIA BLANCO Y CRESPO

That was the name given me at my birth in Seville, Spain in 1775. Because much of my life was spent in England, I was also known as Joseph Blanco White.

My father was a Roman Catholic of Irish descent, and my mother a product of Spanish aristocracy. Father was a struggling merchant who attempted to raise me to follow him in his failing business. My mother encouraged my scholastic pursuits and rejoiced when I announced at the age of 12 that I planned to enter the Catholic priesthood.

For a short time I studied with the Dominicans before transferring to the University of Seville where I was exposed to European literature and the ideas of the enlightenment. Since English had been one of the languages of my home, and used extensively in my father's mercantile business, I became enamored with the translation of English poetry into Spanish. This led into attempting to write poetry of my own, which eventually became my primary vocation.

Upon graduation in 1799 I reluctantly submitted myself to ordination to the priesthood. Reluctant because my introduction into the world of more liberal intellectual thought had seriously eroded the foundations of the dogmas which had seemed so true to me as a young boy.

Nonetheless, I went about my duties, presiding at Mass, preaching, and serving as a chaplain to nuns at a convent to which I had been assigned. More and more I considered religion to be a fable, but I did my best to hide my doubts from others. I was primarily concerned about the possibility of disappointing my mother, but also worried lest I come under the surveillance of the Inquisition.

When Napoleon's troops invaded Spain in 1808 I joined the rebels in Seville, where a provisional Spanish government had been established. I published a political magazine, *El Semanario Patriotico* or *The Patriotic Weekly* in support of the nationalistic uprising. But when I wrote an article critical of what I considered mistakes of the new leaders, the censors forbade me from further publishing.

At that point, in 1810, I left Spain never to return. In England, I took up my writing again, and with financial assistance from the English government published a magazine, *The Spaniard*, which was circulated in Spain until the French were driven out.

In this journal I also began to campaign for freedom of the Americas from Spanish colonization. I began by proposing limited autonomy, but later came to the position that nothing less than complete independence would do. This radical proposition alienated me from the few friends I still had in Spain as they considered me a traitor.

It was also about this time that I learned a secret relationship which I had with Magdalena Esquaya a few years earlier had resulted in the birth of a child. I determined to provide her and my son with financial assistance, which I did until her death several years later. I also later arranged for my son to receive an officer's appointment with the British army.

During these years I also found myself searching for a new understanding of the religious faith I had earlier renounced. I thought I had found it in the Anglican Church. I not only joined the Church of England, but was accepted into the Anglican priesthood on the basis of my prior ordination. I did preach on occasion, but never settled into a parish.

I supported myself through tutoring the sons of English aristocrats, and a continuation of my writing. My descriptions of the life and customs of the Spain of my childhood were published and were hailed as a primary sociological study of that country at the close of the 18th century. This, along with editorship of the magazine *Variedades*, which circulated throughout Latin America brought me both recognition and financial security.

The residue of my relationship with Catholicism was confused, and I am sure confusing. In 1825 I was persuaded by friends to oppose efforts for Catholic Emancipation in England. I wrote that it was not possible to be both tolerant and Catholic. I said the two positions were irreconcilable. But only five years later I spoke in favor of revoking the anti-papal oath which was used to prevent Catholics from seeking public office.

By this time I had joined the faculty at Oxford and was experiencing the same kinds of doubts about Anglicanism which I had earlier harbored about Catholicism. I concluded that the Bible could hardly be a reliable guide to the discovery of religious truths since it was so rife with contradictory teachings. I decided that any Biblical passage which lent itself to a variety of interpretations could not be true. Otherwise God was guilty of deliberately setting traps for the reader. This led, inevitably, to a rejection of the doctrine of the Divinity of Christ. It also, of course, pointed me in the direction of the Unitarians.

I began to attend services to hear Unitarian preachers such as James Martineau and John Hamilton Thom. I entered into correspondence with the American leader, William Ellery Channing. I threw myself without reserve into this new quest for meaning without dogma. I rejoiced in finding a church which did not demand espousal to ideas which in their essence were in opposition to the spirit of Jesus and the Gospels.

My later years were among the most productive of my life. A goodly portion of my finest poetry, both in English and in Spanish, was written in my final decade.

When I died in 1841, I did so thanking God for having been made acquainted with Unitarian worship, having never seen anything superior, or even equal, to it.

But, then, had I lived longer, there is no predicting where I might have been. It was a fundamental premise of my life to never put my opinions on the shelf as if they were settled forever.

Good Morning. I am

JOHN RELLY BEARD

My life spanned the first three-quarters of the 19th century, from my birth in Portsmouth, Hampshire in the year 1800 until my death in 1876. Those of you who know history will recognize that my adult years were lived in the Victorian era.

As a Unitarian minister, my efforts were focused on three major interests. These were extending the outreach of Unitarianism to the working class, educational reform, and internationalism.

I grew up in a working class family of extremely limited income and felt deeply that liberal and liberating religious thought should be the rightful legacy of persons of such conditions.

My thinking on this matter was sharply disputed by others. Persons of such stature in Unitarian circles as my one-time college classmate James Martineau believed that Unitarianism would be severely diminished if not kept in the hands of the more highly educated.

I rejected the advice and counsel of my opponents and was the organizing founder of the Home Missionary Board which trained preachers and established congregations among the lower classes. I firmly believed that if the Unitarian message was to be heard and accepted by those of lesser education and economic status, the message had to be delivered to them by those who emerged from similar circumstances. I served as head of the Board from its formation in 1854 until my retirement twenty years later.

There can be no doubt that this sense of mission came from my own early experiences. My father, as I mentioned, was a common tradesman of limited education. Nonetheless, he was wise enough to extricate himself from the imprisonment of a theology of terror, a God of retribution, and seek out for himself and his family a religion of reason and reconciliation.

The Unitarian minister in Portsmouth took an interest in my welfare and arranged for me to be sent to boarding school in France where I was exposed to a classical education. I returned to enter Manchester College in York to prepare myself for the ministry.

My first settlement was with a small congregation not far from Manchester. The salary the members could pay me was most inadequate, and so, like many other of my ministerial colleagues in similar circumstances, I opened a school to supplement my meager income.

My experiences as a teacher led to the publication of a number of books and articles advocating educational reform. Before long I was deeply involved in efforts to establish a system of universal, non-sectarian, public education. The goals of our campaign were quite similar to those espoused in America by the Unitarian reformer, Horace Mann.

As a minister I always saw myself as a missionary. Now, I know that is language which sounds strange to Unitarian Universalists in the 21st century, but I always believed that if our faith was good enough for us to live by it was good enough to share with others.

While I wrote a goodly number of scholarly books during my career, I left it to others to try to exhibit their scholarship. In everything I did, whether writing or preaching, I always sought to keep the message simple and easily understood. What was to be gained by impressing others with one's great learning if none of that learning was being shared with one's listeners? I dealt with scholarly subjects, but always in a way that was easily accessible to the common man.

One of publications with which I was most satisfied was entitled *Unitarianism Exhibited in its Actual Condition*. This was a collection of articles written by Unitarians in Hungary and America as well as England. It was the first time that these various national expressions of the Unitarian message were presented side by side. It was my attempt to systematically compare and synthesize developing thought on an international scale. It is with great pleasure that I take note of the fact that there is now an International Council of our churches.

I realize now that I have not told you a thing about my family. It would be a serious oversight not to mention my wife, Mary, who mothered our ten children. We were married in an Anglican ceremony because the law required that a Church of England clergyman was necessary to make the marriage legal. We complied with the law, but provided the officiating vicar a written statement protesting the references to the unscriptural doctrine of the Trinity.

I suppose I was always a protester and propagandist by nature. I was never without a "cause" to fight for. More likely two or three at a time. I could never be satisfied with accepting things as they were.

I don't believe I was ever a trouble-maker just for the sake of stirring up controversy. Neither did I ever turn away from doing battle in behalf of the common man.

Those who wished change to come about in a slow and orderly manner considered me a radical. I simply saw myself as one who cooperated with Providence on the side of the dispossessed.

One final word. Unitarian Universalism, as I observe it in your day, remains much too much the possession of the well-educated, well-housed, well-fed upper middle class. That is not true every-where in the world, but in too many places it is. Perhaps it is not too late for you to adopt my passion for taking the message to the working classes of your day. I challenge you to do so.

Good Morning. I am

FLORENCE NIGHTENGALE

My mother and my father, Fanny and William Nightengale, were both staunch Unitarians.

Father was a well-to-do landowner in Embly Park, Hampshire, and as much a radical in his politics as he was in his religion. He was very involved in Wilberforce's campaign to outlaw the slave trade.

Since I was an only child, and there was no male heir, my father lavished his attention on me. He gave me all the privileges that usually fell to an eldest son, including a classic education. I was taught Greek, Latin, French, German, Italian, history and mathematics. Most unusual for a daughter born in 1820.

In direct contrast to this paternal encouragement to grow and blossom in ways of my own choosing, my mother was determined to prepare me to become a lady worthy of my station in life. Her one goal for me, it seemed, was that I marry well.

Later, when I announced that I wished to become a nurse, even my father reversed all he had said and done before and expressed his disapproval. He thought nursing was a task for the lower classes.

I could only conclude that the family is too narrow a field for the development of an immortal spirit, be that spirit male or female. The family uses people. It thinks of them not as what God has made them, but as something which it arranged they should be. It dooms some minds to incurable infancy, and others to silent misery.

My mother was devastated when I refused an offer of marriage from Lord Houghton, and a series of other suitors after him. But I knew that I had a moral and active nature which required satisfaction that I could not find with him, or any other. I was not willing to spend my life in making society and arranging domestic things.

My desire to have a career in medicine was enhanced by a friendship with Elizabeth Blackwell, an American Unitarian, who was the first woman physician in the United States. She had come to St. Bartholomew's Hospital in London. She told me of the opposition and obstacles she had overcome and encouraged me to hold on to my dream. Finally, when I was 31 years of age, my father relented and agreed that I could study nursing.

I enrolled in the Protestant Deaconess Hospital training program in Germany and then returned to work with invalid women in an institution in Harley Street, London.

In 1854, three years after I had begun my studies, the Crimean War broke out. I was appalled by what I read in our English papers of the conditions of our sick and wounded soldiers. I immediately volunteered and was granted permission to take a corps of thirty-eight nurses to the Turkish battle area.

There are no words with which I could convey to you the horror which I encountered there. In our army hospitals only one death in six could be attributed to injuries incurred on the battlefield. The other five died of typhus, cholera, dysentery and other similar causes.

I set out to reform and sanitize the hospitals and upgrade the care given to our fallen boys. You would not believe, if I could adequately tell you, the uproar of opposition that came from the military officers and doctors. They interpreted my desire for humane treatment as personal criticism and an attack on their professional competency.

If I had not had some friendly contacts with editors and journalists in London, nothing would have ever been done. But I was able to convey my concerns to John Delane, the editor of The Times of London. He gave me the opportunity to share with his readers the abominable conditions I had found. An outraged response from the homefront convinced the officers in Crimea to give me permission to make some of the necessary changes in our army hospitals. The death-rate of our patients was dramatically reduced.

I returned to England in 1856 determined to continue my campaign to improve the hygiene and basic medical care of men in the British Army. A long interview with Queen Victoria and Prince Albert proved decisive and resulted in the establishment of the Sanitary Commission and, later, the Army Medical College. The Sanitary Commission was the forerunner of what became the International Red Cross.

People insisted on treating me like a hero. But I always said that I had no peculiar gifts. What I did have was determination. My advice to young women would be the same today as it was then. If you will just try to walk you will soon be able to run the appointed course. But first you must learn to walk. Most people don't even try that. You must qualify yourself for whatever it is you wish to do and never stop trying. Don't even start if you are not willing to finish the race.

Nursing, people told me, is a high calling, an honorable calling. But, I ask you, what does the honor lie in? In working hard during your training to learn and to do all things perfectly. The honor does not lie in putting on nursing like your uniform. Honor lies in loving perfection, consistency, and in working hard for it: in being ready to work patiently: ready to say not "How clever I am!" But, "I am not yet worthy, but I will continue striving to deserve the honor."

One more thing I want to add to my Credo for you before I say goodbye. Most women never have a half-hour in all their lives that they can call their own without fear of offending or of hurting someone. Why do people sit up late, or, more rarely, get up so early? Not because the day is not long enough, but because they have no time in the day just for themselves.

The next time you read some glowing tribute to the Lady with the Lamp, gliding with ethereal beauty down the rows of cots of the wounded soldiers, think instead of the real me. A person of ordinary talents, but fierce and stubborn determination to make a difference no matter what obstacles others might have placed in my way.

Good Morning. I am

BARBARA BODICHON

You asked my Credo, my fundamental belief and life commitment? I believe I expressed it when I was only 22 years of age, in 1849, when I said: "I hope there will be some who will brave ridicule for the sake of common justice to half the people in the world."

I was, of course, talking about justice for women. That was the central, though not the exclusive, mission of my life.

My parentage on my father's side was Unitarian religion and radical politics. For three generations they had served in Parliament. My great grandfather had supported the American Colonists against the British government. My grandfather had worked hand in hand with Wilberforce in his struggle against the slave trade. My father, Benjamin Leigh Smith, carried on their radical tradition as an MP. Another member of the Smith family was Fanny, the mother of Florence Nightengale.

My mother, on the other hand, was from the working class. She was only seventeen, and working as a milliner, when she was seduced by my father and gave birth to me. They never married, but did remain together in a common-law relationship until mother's death from tuberculosis seven years later. I was too young to know any of this, but have been told that it created quite a scandal at the time.

It may seem paradoxical, but Father was a strong supporter of women's rights. He made certain that I received the same education as my brothers in every respect.

It was traditional in that day, in families of means, for sons to be provided with an annual stipend on reaching the age of 21. But my father was determined to treat me equally with my male siblings and granted me a significant yearly allowance.

This permitted me the freedom to pursue my own dreams, which included the establishment of a non-sectarian, co-educational school in London which was open to children of all social and economic classes. This later became the Portman Hall School, which was quite famous in English educational circles.

It was expected, of course, that a young woman should marry. I had many chances. Any daughter of a famous family with significant wealth would not be lacking in ardent suitors. But I had a strong conviction that both the laws of the nation and the customs of society robbed a married woman of her autonomy and personhood. I refused them every one.

In the 1850's, when I was in my middle 20's, I diligently campaigned in behalf of a number of women's issues. I appeared before the House of Commons—most unusual for a woman—to testify in behalf of the legal condition of married women. One of the positive results was an act which allowed divorces to be granted through the courts of law. Prior to this time a woman could attain a divorce only through the process of a Private Act of Parliament. Not only did this Act make it possible for women to escape from abusive relationships, but also protected their property rights when they did so.

I also worked to improve the situation of women in regard to employment. In my book *Women and Work* I spoke strongly for the rights of women to control the money which they earned. The law said that whatever she earned was the property of her husband. Such a degrading idea!

Along with a few like-minded friends, I opened an office which served as an employment placement center for women seeking work. We also sought to open new job opportunities for women wherever we could. As an illustration of the difficulty we faced, listen to this. When it was suggested to a hairdresser that it seemed like a trade suitable for women, he replied: "Impossible, madam. I myself took a fortnight to learn it."

In 1858 I joined with a friend, Bessie Rayner Parkes, to found a journal, *The Englishwoman's Review*. A major concern in the early years of the publication was the extension of higher educational opportunities for women and the right of women to study and practice medicine.

Also, around this time, I met a retired French Army Officer named Eugene Bodichon. He shared my commitment to women's rights and supported me in my efforts which others condemned as radical and unlady-like. I decided things had changed enough that my previous opposition to wedlock was no longer as compelling as it had been before, and we were married.

It was time now in my life to turn my attention almost exclusively to the achievement of women's right to vote. I helped establish, along with other of my Unitarian friends, the Women's Suffrage Committee. We were strongly supported in this effort by John Stuart Mill who presented our petitions to the House of Commons.

I criss-crossed Great Britain again and again lecturing for this cause. Among my most significant accomplishments was the converting and recruiting of Lydia Becker to our ranks. She eventually grew into a position of leadership in this great campaign.

One other major effort demanded my attention and concern. Along with Emily Davies, who had been my partner in so many important ventures across the years, I helped raise funds to establish Girton College. It was the first women's college in Cambridge, and accepted its first students in 1873. A glorious accomplishment! It took another 75 years, however, until 1948, for Girton to be admitted to full membership in the University of Cambridge.

Four years after our college opened I took seriously ill and was rendered invalid until my death in 1891. Even though I could no longer take the active role I had played for the previous three decades, I maintained my active interest to the end.

The struggle had never been an easy one. The obstacles placed in our path by those opposed to change were difficult to overcome. But throughout it all my faith and determination never wavered. I knew our cause was just. And like my sister Unitarian in America, Susan B. Anthony, I knew that failure was impossible.

Good Morning. I am

JOHN ABERNETHY

You might call me a proto-Unitarian. I was certainly Unitarian in my theology even though I was Presbyterian in affiliation. Not a regular Presbyterian, however. I was an early leader in Ireland of the movement known as Non-Subscribers. That means we did not subscribe to the Westminster Confession which was the standard Presbyterian formulation of belief. Or, putting it another way, those of us who were Non-Subscribers were the liberal wing of the Protestant church.

My father was a minister also. He was of Scottish birth and had emigrated to Ulster to serve the congregation of Moneymore in county Londonderry. When James II was overthrown in the Glorious Revolution of 1688 father went to London to pledge his support to the new king, William of Orange.

While he was away riots erupted in Ireland and I was sent to my mother's family in Scotland for safety. There I studied at both Glasgow and Edinburgh before returning to Ireland for my ministerial probation period. In 1703 I was appointed pastor to a congregation in Antrim.

Almost immediately after settling there I organized a group of clergymen from the north of Ireland for the discussion of theology, study of the Scriptures, and debate of issues of church governance. This group later became known as the Belfast Society. Consensus slowly emerged from these men that we should be bound by no power other than the light of Scripture. This was a direct challenge to the autocratic control of the Church leadership. One of our more vociferous opponents said we were "seeking a new light." That was such a perfect description that we were happy thereafter to be called the New Light Movement.

Sometime later the Synod instructed me to assume the ministry of the congregation of Ushers Quay in Dublin. I refused to do so and chose to remain in Antrim in a direct challenge to the authority of the ecclesiastical courts.

A great controversy ensued which involved not only matters of church polity and centralized authority, but also doctrinal issues such as the Trinity and the nature of Jesus. Not surprisingly, those who favored less restrictive church governance also tended to take the more liberal position on theological matters. It was a battle between the Subscribers and the Non-Subscribers. For a period the Non-Subscribing ministers and their congregations were segregated into a separate Presbytery of Antrim. One year later we were all expelled from the Ulster Synod.

Despite this banishment I was invited in 1730 to assume leadership of the Wood Street congregation in Dublin, and this time I moved to our capital city. That congregation was the home of most of the intellectual leaders of Irish Presbyterianism in the 18th century. Its highly influential reputation provided me the opportunity to speak freely on issues of greatest concern to me.

Foremost among these was the civil rights of dissenters. These included not only those of us who were Protestants, but also Catholics and Jews. I strongly opposed, and actively campaigned against, the so-called Test Act which prohibited all who were not members of the Church of England from public office.

Both in public address and in the circulation of printed tracts I denounced all laws that, on account of mere differences of religious opinions and forms of worship, excluded any person of integrity and ability from serving their country.

Jonathon Swift took up his satiric pen against me and branded me and all other dissenters as dangerous fanatics. He wrote that I was "leading the Dregs of the People who should be content with their Mechanical Employments."

I did not consider it fanatic to say that the Anglican Test Act carried the appearance of public censure and distrust or to suggest that men of integrity and ability might be found in all denominations. The members of Parliament disagreed with me, however, and efforts to rescind the law were unsuccessful. That often happens when one is a century or so ahead of his time.

Beyond these civic and ecclesiastical controversies, two basic themes dominated my preaching. The first was the idea that the existence of God is proved by human morality. Everything else is variable. Forms of government, manners of worship; but justice and mercy, gratitude and truth, never alter. The learned and the unlearned equally know this. Every man may look into his own heart and find a standard of right and wrong which is the mark of the Creator on His creatures.

My second recurring theme was the Christian responsibility for reconciliation. The religion of Jesus forbids revenge even against the most grievous wrong. A person has the right to self preservation, but once that has been achieved there can be no further resentment. Even the utmost cruelties ought not to be retaliated. When force is no longer necessary to repel wrong, then the offices of love, forgiveness and reconciliation must take place.

These things I believed with all my heart and soul. Therefore, even though my life seemed to be filled with controversy, I always felt I was guided by an accurate and authentic moral compass and could never harbor animosity toward those who were in disagreement with me.

I died in 1740, at the age of 60, satisfied with a life well-spent.

Top of the morning to you. I am

WILLIAM DRENNAN

I was the proud son of Reverend Thomas Drennan, a minister of the non-subscribing Presbyterian Church in Belfast, Ireland in the middle years of the 18th century. Non-subscribing means that the congregation did not subscribe to the Westminster Confession of Faith with its doctrine of the Trinity. My father preached a religion based on reason and moral philosophy.

It is hardly surprising that I was deeply influenced by him, and found the basis for my radical politics in his advocacy of religious dissent.

Others influenced me as well. John Locke and Joseph Priestley in particular, but none to the extent as my father.

At age 15, in 1769, I was enrolled as a student in Glasgow, Scotland. After graduating with a Liberal Arts degree I began my study of medicine at the University of Edinburgh. With a specialty in obstetrics, I returned to Belfast to establish my practice.

Committed as I was to the healing arts, I could not escape from the larger responsibilities of social reform in the civic arena. I associated myself with a dedicated group of my countrymen who had been inspired to dreams of Irish independence by the revolutionary activities of the American colonists.

We were called the Volunteers, having first been mobilized to protect our homes in the event of a French invasion. We later evolved into an action group for a wide range of needed political reforms.

With the passing years I found the Volunteers much too cautious for my tastes. They seemed satisfied to accept a gradual evolution toward our stated goals. I could not be satisfied with tiny steps when giant strides were needed.

Along with my brother-in-law, Sam McTier, I organized the Society of United Irishmen. Our three-fold mission was the achievement of real independence for Ireland, the establishment of a true republic, and the guarantee of civil and religious rights for all people.

The Society was committed to the achievement of these goals through non-violent means. The government, however, did not believe that. They feared our intentions were less benign.

In 1794 I was arrested and charged with seditious libel for a speech I had delivered to the Dublin chapter of our Society. I had said nothing in that speech to indicate we had any intention of resorting to violence. The authorities, however, presented a case against me based on lies and paid witnesses. I was acquitted only because my lawyer was able to expose the outrageous false testimony of the prosecution's chief witness.

I had prepared a personal statement in my defense, but was not permitted to present it during the trial. After my acquittal, the statement was published. In it I aligned myself with "those Protestants who regard no authority on earth, in matters of religion, save the words and works of its author, and whose fundamental principle is that every person has a right, and in pro-portion to his abilities is under an obligation, to judge for himself in matters of religion; a right subservient to God alone, not a favor to be derived from the gratuitous leniency of government."

Much to my distress and sorrow, the United Irishmen lost faith in the possibility of ever receiving justice through political reform, and turned more and more toward violence and rebellion. I understood their frustration and the sense of despair that led them into the belief that the only hope for success lay in a resort to the use of arms. I could not bring myself go with them. Therefore, I had no part in the uprising of 1798, which ended in disaster for our cause.

Shortly after this I married Sarah Swanwick and moved with her to Shropshire. She was a member of a family of prominent English Unitarians whose friendship and intellectual stimulation gave me great pleasure. After seven years I felt compelled to return to Ireland. I had, by this time, retired from the medical profession, and assumed the editorship of a radical journal, *The Belfast Monthly Magazine.*

With a dedicated group of colleagues I helped establish, in 1810, the Belfast Academical Institution. Our goal was to provide preparatory and college level education to students from both the Catholic and Protestant communities. This was a radical undertaking. Nothing of the kind had ever been attempted before.

We had great dreams that this would become Belfast's first university. Sadly, however, our inability to attract Catholic students doomed our noble experiment to failure.

I have neglected to mention, until now, that I was also a poet. You might have surmised that fact because you know that I was Irish. Are not all Irishmen poets?

The volume of my poetry was limited, but a few of my efforts are well remembered.

In *"When Erin First Rose,"* I wrote:

> Nor one feeling of vengeance presume to defile
> The cause, or the men, of the Emerald Isle.

That was the first published reference to Ireland as the Emerald Isle.

As a fitting climax to my life, at my burial in 1820 my casket was borne by three Protestants and three Catholics. That was the exclamation point at the end of my sentence.

Good Morning. I am

DR. JOSEPH WORKMAN

I was born in the year 1805 in County Antrim, Ireland. All of my family were members of the Presbyterian Church in Dunmurry. It was not an ordinary Presbyterian church however, as our minister leaned in the direction of Arianism. You will recognize that, I am sure, as being very close to Unitarian. In fact, in 1827, which happens to be the year I emigrated to Canada, he and the congregation withdrew agreement to the Westminster Confession and became a part of the Non-Subscribing Church of Ireland. This group had a very close relationship with the British Unitarian movement.

In our new home, Montreal, my brother Benjamin joined me in helping establish a Unitarian Church. Another brother attempted to found another Unitarian congregation in Ottawa, but was not successful. That may have been the only endeavor at which one of the Workman brothers failed.

I studied medicine and became known as the father of Canadian Psychiatry. Another brother founded the Sun Life Insurance Company, and two served as mayors of Montreal and Ottawa. We were a highly motivated clan.

While pursuing a medical degree at McGill University I also taught high school. Later, I joined the faculty of the School of Medicine in Toronto while engaging in the practice of family medicine.

Somehow I also found time and energy to serve as lay preacher of our church, and help write its constitution which affirmed the freedom of private judgment in all matters of faith and declared the complete equality of women and men, with no differentiation in the exercise of privileges.

I had reached the place in my life where I could make such declarations because of the nurturing influence of my wife, Elizabeth Wasnidge Workman, who was as fully committed to the Unitarian way as was I.

My religious beliefs were not limited to individual concerns. As I understood Jesus, his primary interests were in healing the infirm, feeding the hungry, caring for the widows and orphans, and releasing those held in bondage.

That led me to taking leadership roles in the building of a hospital for poor immigrants; advocacy of financial aid to all in poverty; treatment for those suffering from alcoholism or drug abuse; opposition to capital punishment; and giving the franchise to women.

I was particularly interested in working with the mentally ill. Like that wonderful Unitarian woman in America, Dorothea Dix, I worked to get those called insane out of jails and prison cells and into places of humane treatment. I truly believed that doses of human kindness and compassion could reach deep inside them and touch the image of God in which they were created.

Another of my favorite projects was service on the Board of Education, where I strongly supported free public education for all. I advocated non-sectarian education, but will confess that I wanted non-sectarian with an inclination toward Christianity.

I opposed such things as the recitation of the Lord's Prayer to open the school day. But I did believe that the first step in the education process should be impressing on young minds the principles of honesty, truth, benevolence, loyalty to just authority, and resistance to tyranny of oppression of any kind. These, it seemed to me, were the primary Christian virtues.

After those great ideas were taught, the educator could turn to teaching those insights and skills which were necessary in the pursuit of the daily necessities of living and other refinements.

I said, again and again, that the exclusion of females from the study of the more profound branches of literature and science was nothing less that barbaric.

While being fully committed to the work of our Unitarian Church, I had great difficulty in harboring any patience for other churches which majored in religious commotion which drove emotionally unstable people into a form of guilt-induced insanity. I saw too many preachers who were nothing other than hookers of money, rather than fishers of men or shepherds to the flock. I found very little of Christ in what paraded itself about wearing the name of Christianity.

Our Unitarian Church in Montreal grew and flourished with the passing years. Early on I pledged that as long as God spared my life and gave me health, I would never forsake that congregation no matter what trials of fire it would be forced to endure. I never wavered from that declaration.

That doesn't mean that I was always confident and secure in my religious beliefs. Oh, on the contrary! My mind was constantly teeming with questions and doubts. But that is why I was Unitarian. I could not have existed in a society which did not permit, indeed encourage, the free exercise of private judgment in all these matters.

In fact, I went to my death in 1894, at the age of 89, determined to engage in a dialogue with the Deity over why, when He chose to make man, He did not choose to make him whole. I understood why He chose against perfection, but to make man with so fragile a thing as the human mind was, to me, incomprehensible.

I won't tell you what I have learned. That would spoil the rest of your adventurous journey.

Good Morning. I am

JOHN CORDNER

Friends have said that I was the most prominent, and important, leader of the Unitarian movement in Canada in the 19th century. While I appreciate the accolade, I can think of many others whose contribution was equal, if not superior, to mine. The Workman brothers, for example, who founded our churches in Montreal, Ottawa and Toronto. I think, also, of people like Emily Stowe, Elizabeth Cushing, and John Young. They are more worthy of praise than am I. Perhaps, I have been singled out because I served as minister of the congregation in Montreal for thirty-five years, from 1843 until 1878.

I did not start out as a Unitarian. Nor, for that matter, as a Canadian. Ireland was my place of birth and the Presbyterian Church was my cradle-faith. Neither was a life in the ministry my original intent. I made that decision after I was fully grown and had been a man of business for several years. The controversy in the church over the orthodoxy of the Westminster Confession which resulted in the liberals being ousted from fellowship in 1829 was the defining incident for me. This brought about the organization of the Non-Subscribing wing of Presbyterianism. I chose the ministry, and I cast my lot with those who were being called "the Irish Unitarians." The ones who used those words about us did not intend them as a compliment.

In 1842 Joseph and Benjamin Workman established the Christian Unitarian Society in Montreal. Since they, and many of the other founding members, had emigrated to Canada from Ireland, they looked back to their native land to secure pastoral leadership. A year after the establishment I accepted their invitation to become the minister. Since my ordination had been from the Remonstrant Synod of Ulster the congregation accepted ties to that organization. It was not until my thirty-five years of service were completed that the church became a part of the American Unitarian Association.

I considered myself a Biblical preacher. I opposed the doctrine of the Trinity because it was not Biblical. I looked upon Jesus as both a revelation of the loving nature of God and as an ethical model for human behavior. I preached that nothing could be considered true theology if it was contradictory to human reason and scientific knowledge.

Totally behind me were the Calvinistic ideas of my youth which taught that eternal punishment awaited all but the "elect" of God. I taught that each of us had to take personal responsibility for our individual sins. And, that if punishment was necessary it would be proportionate to the nature and gravity of the offense. But the concept of eternal punishment was unthinkable.

In all of these things I was condemned as an infidel by those out-side our movement and as overly conservative by many members of my own Unitarian Society. I was certainly no trailblazer on the theological frontier.

Perhaps it was in the arena of social action that others saw me as a pioneer.

My arrival in Canada coincided with the Great Potato Famine in Ireland in which more than a million died of starvation and perhaps twice that number emigrated to the United States and Canada. I considered my recent elevation to a position of influence in Montreal a sign from Providence that I was to do all within my power to ease their suffering.

As the United States moved inexorably toward Civil War over the issue of slavery, I felt under moral obligation to discourage Canadian merchants from supporting the slave-holding southern states for their own economic benefit. Beyond that local effort, I also distributed pamphlets throughout both England and Canada urging support for Abolition.

I added my voice to the chorus of the Suffragists campaigning for a woman's right to vote. In this I was supporting a number of the women members of our congregation who were leaders in this struggle.

I opposed the death penalty; called for reformation of the penal system; and worked to get the insane out of prisons and into human treatment centers.

So persistent was I in my call for morality in the social order that some compared me to an Old Testament prophet. I was enough of a Biblical scholar to know that the prophets were not particularly popular among those they sought to reform.

But it was clear to me that one after another ancient civilizations had fallen into ruin because of internal corruption, materialism, and disregard of the poor. Canada was not immune to these very sins. And if that meant that I had to call into question the behavior of Prime Minister John MacDonald, then that was what I had to do. And I did!

Another time, when the Prince of Wales was planning to visit Montreal, elaborate arrangements were made for an expensive banquet in his honor. From my pulpit I petitioned the city fathers to forego the dinner and use the money for a farm on which vagrant boys could be sheltered and taught trades. Needless to say, the city fathers disagreed.

Meanwhile our congregation grew and flourished. A few complained that I seemed to spend too much time on civic matters and too little on pastoral concerns. Nonetheless, it was my belief, and one shared by the majority of our congregants, that the church should not only seek to influence its own members, but also the total community of which it is a part. The church should be the yeast in the lump which influences the whole.

After thirty-five years of ministry, my health failed and I was forced to retire. Not wishing to remain nearby and interfere with the one who was to follow me, my wife and I moved to Boston where I lived out the remaining 12 years of my life.

Good Morning. I am

DR. EMILY JENNINGS STOWE

My Credo is very short and to the point. It was the business of my life to see that doors were opened, that women might have the same opportunities as men.

Now, I suppose I should proceed to tell you how I came to have that mission for my life and how I acted on it for many, many years.

A social conscious was part of my heritage. I was born into a Quaker home in Upper Canada in the year 1831. Quakers, more than others, tended to cherish education for daughters as well as sons, and I received academic training that was not available to many other girls of my time.

I grew up to become a schoolteacher, and even achieved rank of principal of a school. That was a first for a Canadian woman. And, by the way, only the first of my many "firsts" over the next half century.

When I was 25 I married John Stowe who was both a carpenter and a part-time Methodist minister. Only a few years later John became ill with tuberculosis and I was faced with the responsibility of supporting myself and three small children.

Finding this nearly impossible on the small salary of a schoolteacher, I determined to study medicine and become a doctor. I was refused admission to the University of Toronto because I was a woman. With sacrificial help from my family, I crossed our southern border and enrolled at the New York City Medical College for Women.

Two years later, in 1867, I returned to Toronto to pursue my practice, but was refused a license. They said it was because their rules prohibited the licensing of anyone who had studied in another country. But I had only studied in another country because they would not permit me to study in Canada because I was—well, you know why!

I practiced medicine nonetheless. In the face of every possible kind of opposition, threats of fines and imprisonment, I put to use the knowledge and the skill I had received in the alleviation of human sickness and suffering.

We come now to the question of whether or not I was the first Canadian female physician. The first females to practice medicine in what we call North American were, of course, Native Americans. But if you specify Canadian women most biographers have hailed me as number one. But that honor may belong to my friend and co-worker Jennie Kidd Trout.

She came along a few years later, but was officially certified by the Ontario Medical Association five years before they relented and granted me a license.

Only three years after I was certified to practice, which I had been doing for a quarter of a century, I helped organize the Women's Medical College in Toronto to keep others from having to travel the tortuous path that I had been forced to endure.

By this time, John had recovered from his illness and decided to study dentistry. After his graduation we opened a partnership and practiced together.

All the time I had been getting more deeply involved in the full spectrum of the struggle for women's rights. Just as Elizabeth Cady Stanton and Susan B. Anthony were campaigning in nearby New York, Canadian women were waging their own struggles in behalf of the same issues.

I fought to gain the right of married women to own property and control their own financial affairs. I lobbied for legislation to gain improved working conditions for women in factories. I campaigned to gain admission for women in the nation's universities and graduate schools. I worked for prison reform and humane treatment for the insane.

Most of all I involved myself in the fight for the right to vote. I was a founding member of the Toronto Women's Literary Club which was a euphemistic name for a determined band of women with a radical political agenda.

Susan B. Anthony invited me to join her in Washington, DC in 1883 for a meeting of the International Council of Women. She convinced me that our name needed to be made more specific and we became the Canadian Suffrage Organization, and I served as its president.

I told our members to expect opposition and unpopularity. That is a price that is always paid by those who challenge the status quo. It has always been a hard matter to get out of old ruts and make new furrows. Those who would be deterred by public derision clearly are not fit for membership. But the strength we found in our common sisterhood gave us the courage to survive and overcome.

For most of my life I was an active member of the Unitarian Church in Toronto. Often I meditated on the fact that both Miss Anthony in the United States and I in Canada had been born into the Society of Friends and found the mature expression of our faith in action as Unitarians. That is surely more than an accident of history.

When I was 72 years of age, two years after the death of my husband, John, I suffered a disabling accident which forced me to give up my active professional and civic life. But by this time my daughter, Augusta Stowe Cullen, had succeeded me in both the medical profession and in the social action and political arena. If I may say so, she surpassed her mother in every regard. Would you expect a mother to say anything other than that?

One more thing I want you to know about my life. When I died in 1903 I left instructions with the minister of our Unitarian Church that I wanted my body to be cremated. That was very uncommon in those days. But I did not want to further pollute the earth.

I had not been sufficiently discreet in my discussing my emerging ideas with my friends and classmates. Shortly after the purge began one of my so-called friends . . . I never found out for sure which one . . . reported to the authorities about ideas I had expressed in private conversations. I was arrested, charged with blasphemy, and remanded to the Tolbooth Prison.

I was charged under the provisions of an act which decreed death for anyone who cursed or denied God.

When I was brought to trial, five men, all of whom I had considered friends and confidantes, came forward as witnesses for the prosecution. Among the things they reported having heard me say were:

+ That theology was nothing more than a rhapsody of feigned and invented nonsense.

+ That I had called the Old Testament nothing other than "Ezra's Fables."

+ That I had called the New Testament "the history of the imposter Christ who had learned magic in Egypt and picked up a following of a few ignorant fishermen."

Whether I actually made those statements or not is of no consequence at this point in time. Perhaps I did. Perhaps I did not. It doesn't really matter now.

But my "friends" were certainly correct when they said I had denied the doctrine of the Trinity and said it was too foolish an idea to be even worthy of contradiction.

And, maybe, I did say on occasion when I was freezing in the cold Scottish winters that I would not mind being warmed in hell. No defense was offered at my trial. I had no advocate to speak for me. No notice was taken of the fact that I was a first-time offender and thus subject to a lesser verdict than death.

Good Morning. I am

BJORN PETURSSON

I was born and educated in Iceland, but emigrated to western Canada as a relatively young man. I was a part of a mass migration to North America by at least 20% of Iceland's citizens during the last three decades of the 19th century. Many of us settled in the American states of Minnesota and North Dakota. Others, like myself, moved to Manitoba and Saskatchewan.

Unlike many immigrant groups, we Icelanders were a well-educated and highly independent-minded people. Religiously we were Lutherans, but with a difference. For centuries our Christianity had been intermixed with the images and metaphors of Norse mythology. Most of us had long since given up the idea that Christianity was an exclusive path to the knowledge of God.

Leaving our homeland and moving to new countries brought not only a sense of physical dislocation, but also of spiritual rootlessness. The Lutheran churches we found in both Canada and the United States were much more conservative than those we had known before. Many attempted to become assimilated in the new culture by adopting the dogma of the congregations they found. Others of us were left adrift, being unable to accept what we thought were outmoded and irrelevant doctrines and practices.

In my youth in Iceland I had received some theological training, then entered politics and served a term in Parliament, before settling down as a farmer in Manitoba.

Almost by accident—a most fortunate accident—I discovered an advertisement in a newspaper, placed by the Post Office Mission of the Unitarians of Minnesota. Not knowing exactly what to expect in return, I responded to the ad. The ensuing result was something I could never have anticipated.

I was sent printed materials describing the Unitarian way of religious searching. I was introduced to a concept of free enquiry as practiced by Felix Adler and the Ethical Culture Societies.

Best of all, I was introduced to Jennie McCaine who was secretary of the Post Office Mission, and who, in due time, became my wife.

Kristofer Janson, the Norwegian-born minister of the Unitarian Church in Minneapolis, took a special interest in us. He not only translated a number of Unitarian tracts into Norwegian but arranged for them to be printed and distributed by the American Unitarian Association.

All of this was taking place at a time when, according to the national census of 1881, there were only 25 persons who identified themselves as Unitarians between Toronto and British Columbia. We were sowing seeds on virgin land, indeed.

Two years after Jennie and I were married we moved to Winnipeg, with the financial support of the AUA, and began holding Unitarian services. In February 1891 the First Icelandic Unitarian Church of Winnipeg was established with 22 founding members.

Even though I was the official minister, Jennie filled the pulpit on Sunday mornings almost as frequently as I.

The message was always presented in a reserved and dignified manner, as was befitting our individual personalities. Neither of us were given to bold oratory or disputation. We simply presented a picture of a human Jesus who was a child of God in the same way that all persons are children of God. It was only because of his purity of heart and total devotion of spirit that he should be accepted as a model for all humans to follow. Living a moral and ethical life and working for justice in society was more important than what a person believed. Every individual was responsible for creating his or her own belief-system based on one's personal understanding.

The established Lutherans could not contain their anger at what they considered our heresy. Jennie and I were branded "the paid tools of American infidelity, laboring zealously toward the goal of unchristianizing Canada."

I sought not to respond in kind, but with logic and reason. They claimed we had no faith in God. I said that if Unitarians believed that God would not condemn a single soul to eternal damnation, we had more faith in God than any other group of Christians.

I also responded by suggesting that if Christianity consisted of following the moral and ethic teachings of Jesus, then Unitarians were prime practitioners of the Christian faith.

Our growth was never spectacular, but it was steady. Eighteen months after our founding we moved into a new building which had been made possible by a grant from the American Unitarian Association. On Christmas Day 1892 we held our first service in the new church building.

Less than a year later I took ill and died at the age of 67. For the next year Jennie carried on as minister, until a suitable replacement could be found.

With the arrival of Reverend Magnus Skeptason, who had been expelled by his synod for expressing Universalist views, Jennie returned to her native New Hampshire for the remainder of her life.

When the cornerstone of our church was opened in 1962 it was found to contain a volume of poems by Bjorn Gunnlaugsson which refuted the doctrine of a God of vengeance. They found a hymn book, written by Magnus Stephensen, one-time Chief Justice of Iceland, which deleted all references to the devil. They found verses composed by the poet and statesman Jon Olafsson who had often preached there.

It was a great heritage, indeed. I am so grateful I had a part in the expansion of Unitarianism to the Canadian west and for being a part of the Icelandic culture which brought such rich diversity to its development.

Good Morning. I am

VILHJALMUR STEFANSON

At one time I considered becoming a Unitarian minister but changed directions and became an anthropologist and Arctic explorer instead. I did, however, remain a Unitarian throughout my entire life.

I was born in the year 1879 in a remote village in an area called New Iceland in the far northern reaches of Manitoba. My parents were both immigrants from Iceland, but in order to display their acceptance of their new life in Canada, christened me with the English name William. Later, to reestablish my own identity, I adopted the Icelandic form Vilhjalmur.

The year after my birth a flood devastated our village and its surroundings, and the family found another new home, this time in North Dakota. Life was hard. Survival was difficult. But like others of that time and place we persevered without complaint.

I had very little formal education, but did have a thirst for knowledge. About the only book that was available was the Bible, and it became the textbook I read and studied at every possible opportunity.

Through sporadic correspondence with relatives and friends in Winnipeg my parents knew of the establishment of the Icelandic Unitarian Church. As inheritors of the same spirit of free enquiry they embraced this faith as their own.

My father died while I was quite young and I moved to the home of an older sister. There I helped support my mother and the other children as a cowboy and horse trader.

At 17 I enrolled in a preparatory academy of the University of

North Dakota. After two years I was expelled for having helped organize a campus protest. The details are not really important. It was only a minor one of many protests I engaged in during my long and public life. After that I enrolled in the University of Iowa and received a bachelor's degree in 1903.

A few years earlier, while still in North Dakota, I had become acquainted with Samuel Eliot, who was president of the American Unitarian Association. He had, at that time, told me that he thought I exhibited qualities of mind and spirit that would make a good Unitarian minister. He even went so far as to offer to pay my expenses at Harvard Divinity School if I were inclined to pursue that calling.

I contacted Dr. Eliot and informed him that I was ready to accept his prior offer if it was still valid. He quickly made all necessary arrangements and I was soon a student in Cambridge.

In addition to my theological studies, I also enrolled in as many classes in anthropology as possible. As more of a humanist than a theist, I sensed that the study of humankind was more "religious" than the study of metaphysics.

In 1906 I left the Divinity School to join an expedition to explore the Arctic. This was, as you know, three years prior to Peary's setting foot on the North Pole. My primary interest, however, was not in geography, but in the people who inhabited this region of the earth. I never actually made contact with the expedition, but rather, on my own, spent the winter months living with the Inuits learning to hunt and fish in the way they had learned over the centuries.

After this life-centering experience, I persuaded the American Museum of Natural History in New York to underwrite a second expedition. I teamed up with a friend from the University of Iowa, Rudolph Anderson, to travel to the northern reaches of Alaska for a study of native language and culture. We spent two years on this venture.

One fascinating discovery was an isolated colony of Inuits whose facial features were decidedly more European than Asian, which led me to the conclusion that they were probably descendants of Vikings who had sailed to that region many centuries before.

A third expedition, in 1913, which took us from Victoria to Nome and on to the western Arctic Ocean, ended in controversy. I had gone on alone, as was my usual practice, when our boat, Karluk, sank with considerable loss of both life and physical resources.

After that disappointment, coupled with the onset of World War I, I turned my attentions to academic matters. I published the findings of my anthropological studies in a number of scientific journals, and in popular form in my book *My life with the Eskimo*. I really wanted the world to know the remarkable people I had found living in what I came to recognize as the "friendly Arctic" and the "hospitable north."

It seemed to me that people in Canada and the United States were burdened with stereotypical ideas about the Arctic as a desolate, wind-swept land sparsely occupied by backward primitive people. I wanted them to know the beauty of that land and the intricate social systems those gifted indigenous people had developed over the years.

In my efforts to achieve that goal I published two other books, *The Story of Five Years in Polar Regions* and *The Northwest Course of Empire*.

The newly established Pan American Airline called on me to help them chart over-the-pole flight lanes. Charles Lindbergh conferred with me in preparation for his historic trans-Atlantic solo flight. During World War II, I helped educate the Alaska Defense Force on survival tactics in the region. Engineers sought my advise on mapping the Alaska Highway.

I made my living writing and lecturing, and was a frequent speaker at Unitarian Churches across Canada.

115

My final years were spent in Hanover, New Hampshire where I continued my research, writing and lecturing at Dartmouth College.

My wife, Evelyn and I, remained active with the Unitarian Fellowship until I set out on my final expedition of discovery in 1962, my death.

Good Morning. I am

JOSEPH T. THORSON

I was associated almost from my birth in 1889 with the Icelandic Unitarian movement in my native Manitoba. Precepts learned in that community guided me throughout a long career in politics and law.

When a legal dispute arose in 1919 over the ownership of property known as the Tabernacle in Winnipeg, I offered my services to the Unitarian side of the conflict. The building had originally been constructed and owned by the Lutherans, but over a period of years those of Unitarian leanings had gained majority status. Interrelated to this was the nearly twenty year ministry of F. J. Bergmann, a man of decidedly liberal theology and great personal charm. He was ex-communicated by the Lutheran Synod, but was backed by his congregation of nearly 2,000 members and remained in firm control for another decade.

Upon his retirement the Lutherans went to court to reclaim the property. It fell to me to convince the judge that the property should remain in the hands of those who worshiped there. I lost the case when the judge ruled that the Tabernacle should revert to its original owners. Many of the Unitarians wanted to appeal the verdict. I said that they would be wiser to use their money on a new building rather than on legal fees in what would probably be a losing cause. They took my advice and created the First Icelandic Federated Church, comprised of Unitarians and liberal Christians.

A year later I was named the first Dean of the Law School at the University of Manitoba. I served in that position for five years before making my initial entrance into politics. As a member of the Liberal Party I ran, and was elected, to the Canadian Parliament.

Four years later, in 1930, I was defeated in a bid for reelection. I learned from that defeat and came back to successfully be elected again for two additional terms.

While serving as a Member of Parliament I got involved in a very interesting case back home in Manitoba. The B'nai B'rith wanted to purchase land to build a summer camp on the shores of Lake Winnipeg in Gimli. Almost every property owner in the area signed a petition claiming the land was "for gentiles only." I was able to keep the matter out of court by convincing enough of the petitioners to withdraw their opposition that the Gimli Town Council approved the sale and the construction of the camp. I was pleased to have the opportunity to strike a blow for justice.

Also during this time I served as a Canadian delegate to the League of Nations. It was my ill-fortune to be a close-up observer of the impotence of that international organization to forestall either Mussolini's invasion of Ethiopia or Hitler's takeover of Austria. That was a most distressing period of my life.

At the outbreak of World War II, I became a member of the Cabinet, serving first as Minister of National War Services and later as Minister of National Mobilization. Always an independent person who marched to his own drummer, I was frequently at odds on matters of policy with Prime Minister Mackenzie King. He solved that problem by appointing me to the presidency of the Exchequer Court of Canada.

During the decade of the 1950's I served as president of the International Commission of Jurists. This is a non-governmental organization which works to promote the rule of law and the legal protection of human rights throughout the world. It came into being in response to the UN Universal Declaration of Human Rights. That document says: "It is essential if Humankind is not to be compelled to have recourse, as a last resort, to rebellion against tyranny and oppression, that human rights should be protected by the rule of law."

In the early 60's I turned my attention to the danger of the prolif-
eration of atomic weaponry and its potential for the destruction of
humanity. I became president of the Canadian Campaign for
Nuclear Disarmament. Admittedly, Canada was not one of the
powers engaged in the nuclear race, but we felt an obligation,
both moral and selfish, to add our voices to the plea for sanity and
restraint.

The last great battle of my life was for the preservation of a united
Canada. Quebec's campaign for independence was most
disturbing to me. It was not that I was antagonistic to those of
French extraction who felt their rights were not being sufficiently
protected. It was just that I wanted, oh so deeply, for those defi-
ciencies to be corrected in a united country.

I campaigned strenuously for a single Canada in which all our
citizens, regardless of ethnic origin, whether British or French, or
neither British nor French, could stand on equal footing with one
another . . . both in the enjoyment of their rights and in the
fulfillment of their duties, without any preferential treatment to
the members of any component of the Canadian nation.

Canada, I believed, had never accepted the melting pot theory of
assimilation. We had welcomed all those who had helped build
our country and left them free to hold in affectionate regard the
memories and traditions of the lands from which they came. This
regard for the individual and absence of compulsion had been a
fundamental Canadian policy.

It was certainly true of my Icelandic forebears. I wanted it to be
true for all others as well.

It was very painful to know that some interpreted my position as
being anti-French Canadian. This simply was not so.

What I wanted for my beloved country was what I had learned in
my Unitarian Sunday School: appreciation and respect for the
dignity of every individual and the essential unity of the entire
human family.

Good Morning. I am

DOROTHY LIVESAY

I was a poet, a social activist, an officer in the Order of Canada, and a Unitarian Universalist.

Born in Winnipeg, Manitoba my life covered all but the first nine and the final four years of the twentieth century.

My parents were both very remarkable and talented people, and, I thought, terribly unsuited to one another. They were both writers. They met, in fact, when on the staff of the *Winnipeg Telegram*. Mother was a very proper person and always made sure that I never missed a Sunday service at the Anglican Church. Father, on the other hand, was a delightfully mischievous agnostic.

They both, in their own individual ways, encouraged me toward a literary career. When I was 13 my mother discovered some poetry I had written, but had shown to no one other than my closest friend. She submitted my writings to a newspaper for publication. I was absolutely devastated. My privacy had been invaded and my inmost thoughts made public. My anger subsided, however, when the newspaper sent me a check in the amount of $2.00 for publishing my work.

Father's way of encouragement was to give me a copy of *A Room of One's Own* with the inscription, "Go thou and do likewise!"

In my teen years we moved to Toronto where I attended the university and, at 19, published my first volume of poetry, *Green Pitcher*. Twenty-five others followed during the next half century.

College was followed by a year of graduate study at the Sorbonne in Paris. It was my intention to return to Canada and teach, but the Great Depression changed those plans. Unable to find a teaching position I turned to social work. This exposure to the misery and abject poverty of the urban unemployed, and particularly the suffering of women and children, led me to an acceptance of Marxism as an antidote to the evils of capitalism.

I moved to Vancouver and became a writer for a left-wing journal. It was there I met Duncan McNair whom I married in 1937. During the next four years we had two children, a boy and a girl, and I adjusted myself to marriage and motherhood.

All the while I grew increasingly disenchanted with the Communist Party and withdrew from it. I remained, however, a Socialist. I blame myself for having been duped by the Communists, but cannot forget that in the 30's they seemed to be the only ones who were concerned about the plight of the unemployed and minorities; and the only ones seemingly aware of the threat of Hitler and a coming war.

It was about this time, also, that Duncan and I found the Unitarian Church. I had been brought up, as I mentioned earlier, in an orthodox religious atmosphere. But in my college days I began to seriously question Anglican dogma. I found a very free spirit of enquiry into the historical origins of Judaism and Christianity. This made it easier for me to repudiate orthodox religion and to substitute a deterministic, Marxist, view of the origin of man.

Paradoxically, at the same time I was embracing economic determinism, I was also taking delight in a study of the 17th century poets—all of whom were not writing in praise of man, but for the greater glory of God!

Preaching one time at the Unitarian Church in Vancouver I explained how I missed "the sense of the mysteriousness of life," and criticized the common tendency among Unitarians to adopt a completely rationalistic and humanistic stance. Instead of ignoring the possibility of an outside power as the source of human creativity, we should be making a study of these matters.

The deterministic concept does not go far enough. It ignores vast areas of human experience which cannot be ignored: I mean the areas of intuition, creativity and mysticism. What I was pleading for was poetic insight, such as that of Donne, Blake, Whittier, and Emily Dickinson.

I once wrote in my journal: "I feel that the beauty of the natural world and the artist's or poet's revelation of it does lead to inner harmony-peace-truth. The Gothic cathedrals do lift us out of time."

After Duncan's death I returned to Paris to work for UNESCO, and that led to a position at a teacher training college in Northern Rhodesia just as it was making the transition to the independent nation of Zambia.

What a marvelous experience that was for me. All through the 30's I had fought for a changed society. Then came World War II and Korea. Now, at last, I was witnessing the miracle of a complete rebirth. I saw the colonial chains fall away and a new society emerge. It was a great psychic release for me to be so close to these people who were changing their society. That was what led to the writing of *The Colour of God's Face*, which I consider my finest work.

The experience in Africa was transforming for me in many ways. Not only was I deeply gratified to see at such close range the glory of a people gaining freedom, but I was liberated within myself.

I found a new freedom in personal expression. I discovered and maintained a cadence of life which forever seemed to be synchronized with the rhythms of African drums. As I grew older, my poetry grew more sensual. I wrote of nakedness, which was my metaphor for honesty. And honesty is the essence of my Credo.

Good Morning. The name given to me at my birth is

MOODELLIAR VELLZHA

The year is not known. It was sometime in the 1770's, during the Hyder rebellion near the southeastern tip of India. Both of my parents were killed in that uprising and I was raised by relatives. It was our lot that we were low-caste Tamil Hindus, and we lived accordingly.

If you have ever heard of me, it would have been by the name William Roberts which I adopted when I was baptized a Christian at a much later date.

Sometime before my tenth birthday I moved to Madras to seek work. There I was captured by a Muslim trader who sold me into slavery to a European ship owner. Later the man who owned me died and the captain of the ship made me a regular employee. He even paid me back wages for the time I was enslaved. He later gave me employment in his own home in England.

It was there that I learned English, became acquainted with the Bible and the Anglican Book of Common Prayer, and was baptized a Christian. In 1789, when I was probably in my late teenage years, I returned to Madras as the servant of another English gentleman.

I diligently continued my study of the Scriptures and the Prayer Book. For me, the Athanasius Creed was incomprehensible. It simply did not seem possible to me that God and the Lord had the same attributes but were separate, and still were only one God. My uneducated mind could not unravel that mystery. Neither did I have the wisdom at that time to read the Bible without the Book of Common Prayer. Therefore, I did not know how greatly the Scriptures had been corrupted.

Four years later I returned to England. A young woman who served as a maid in a household in which I was employed knew of my interest in religious matters and gave me some writings of the Unitarian ministers Theophilus Lindsey and Joseph Priestley. I returned to Madras with a sizeable library of Unitarian books which I read with great care.

I made one final trip to England in 1806. It was my desire to meet face to face with the Reverend Thomas Belsham, minister of the Unitarian Society in London, with whom I had carried on extensive correspondence. Also I wished to meet Reverend Lindsey whose works I had read so avidly. But when given the opportunity to meet with such important and educated personages, I avoided doing so because of my low estate in life.

Back home again in Madras I set out to organize a Unitarian community. The task was arduous, but I never flagged in my determination. Over the next two decades a significant Unitarian presence was established in our section of the Indian subcontinent.

Time and time again, I pleaded with our English counterparts for aid. We asked for funds, for educational materials, and most of all for an English missionary who would give us ministerial leadership.

Reverend Belsham did offer some limited financial assistance and a bountiful supply of printed materials, but did not agree that an English missionary would be either desirable or possible. He said that I should train two or three young people who would be much more qualified to instruct their own countrymen.

He further wrote that he not only considered it unwise to send a missionary to India, but that he doubted it would be possible to find any English Unitarian who would undertake such an enterprise. This saddened me deeply. I saw all around me the missionaries who represented the Baptists, Methodists and

Moravians. Why, I wondered, were there no Unitarians who would do the same?

Nevertheless, our little congregation grew in both numbers and in spirit. Our school flourished and served a great purpose in providing education to many in our area who would otherwise have had no school. Our children were not allowed to attend either Muslim schools or those for upper-caste Hindus.

Of course, we remained suspect in the eyes of our Hindu neighbors as well as other Christian churches. About the most kind thing any said about us was to call our rational religion "refined heathenism."

Our congregation was made up of men who worked as gentlemen's servants, butlers, cooks, and cook's mates. Three were drummers in the service of the Nabob, and three were teachers. The women mostly worked in their homes taking care of their children. Almost all of the men could read and write and a few of the women as well. Many of them had been able to purchase their own Bibles and read it aloud in their homes.

Our activities in Madras were regularly reported in Unitarian journals in both London and Boston. My repeated requests for a missionary to be sent to us stirred up considerable controversy in both countries. Most agreed with Belsham that complying with my request would be unwise, but others argued that if Unitarianism was worth believing it ought to be worth propagating.

You must remember that all this took place before Unitarian Associations were firmly established in either England or America. I am confident they did for us what seemed provident to them at that time.

There were other outposts of Unitarianism in other areas in India, but none have stood the test of time as did ours. Elsewhere the movement flowered, then withered and died. This was so even in Calcutta where the assistance of an English minister was available. The work in Madras continues to this day.

It may well be that what I considered indifference to our plight was the best thing that could have happened to us. I truly believed, at that time, that we needed English leadership. When they refused to send someone I feared it was because we were of low estate and another race.

But, perhaps, it was because they did not wish to engage in paternalism. Perhaps, in their wisdom they saw it was best for us to not be dependent on others. Perhaps they knew we would have a better chance to survive if we were forced to develop our own indigenous, native leadership. Perhaps that is why we have continued to this very day.

Good Morning. I am

RAM MOHUN ROY BAHADOOR

Some have called me the Father of Modern India.

I was born of Brahman parents in the village of Radhanagar in the year 1772 during the time of British rule in Bengal. My father was of the lineage of the renowned 16th century Vishnu reformer, Caitania. We were a prosperous family of a privileged caste.

Early in my life I exhibited many unorthodox ideas about religion which were the occasion of conflict within the family. After my father's death my mother attempted, without success, to have me disinherited on the charge of apostasy.

Separated, and alienated, from my family, I supported myself through a variety of financial ventures. I managed small estates, engaged in money lending, and speculated in bonds of the British East India Company.

During this formative period of my life I immersed myself in the study of western literature and culture. This stimulated much serious comparison of the religions of the world. That led me to renounce the superstitions and irrationality I found in all of them. Instead, I came to advocate natural religion in which we are guided by reason to the Absolute Originator, the first principle of all religions, but who is beyond human knowledge.

In the busy first two decades of the 19th century I published vernacular English summaries of the Vedanta Sutras, an ancient Sanskrit religious treatise, as well as Bengali and Hindi translations of the Kena, Isa, Katha, Mandukya and Mundaka Upanishads. In each I emphasized the unknowable Supreme God who supports the universe. In so doing I established a reputation both as a modern exponent of the Vedanta School of Hindu philosophy and as a nonconformist. I did not consider myself a reformer, even though others placed me in that camp. The French Societe Asiatique honored me in 1824 by electing me to honorary membership in recognition of my translations.

Several Baptist missionaries approached me and together we began work on a Bengali translation of the New Testament. Foremost among them was William Adam, a native of Scotland, who was a distinguished Biblical scholar and linguist. Our work of translation was disrupted by a dispute over the divinity of Jesus. For me, the issue was the same as with my Hindu critics. I argued for the Oneness of God.

Somewhat surprisingly, Adam sided with me in this dispute with his fellow Baptists. He, henceforth, declared himself a Unitarian, and established relationships with Unitarian societies in both England and America.

My interest in Christianity was focused on the moral character of the teachings of Jesus. In 1820 I published *Precepts of Jesus. The Guide to Peace and Happiness*, a treatise on the ethical teachings of the Gospels.

Adam and a few other European friends joined me in forming the Calcutta Unitarian Society. He appealed to his fellow Unitarians in Britain and America for support for our venture. What little came in response to his plea was too late and too meager to be of much help.

In addition to my religious enquiries, I was also involved in numerous social issues of Indian society. I traveled to England to intercede with the government in behalf of the abolition of sati, the ritual death of widows on the funeral pyres of their husbands.

While in Britain I was warmly received by the Unitarians, particularly Dr. Lant Carpenter, distinguished minister of the large congregation in Bristol. His young daughter, Mary, later made a great contribution to India through the establishment of schools for girls.

Education was a major concern of mine, too. I founded both the Anglo-Hindu School and Vedanta College. When the government of Bengal sought to establish a Sanskrit college which would feature the teaching of classic Indian literature I protested, saying that such a narrow education would not adequately prepare Bengali youth for the challenges of the modern world.

When the British imposed censorship on the press in Calcutta, I spoke from the vantage point of my editorship of two weekly newspapers. I appealed to the spirit of both the American and French Revolutions and claimed freedom of speech and religion as natural rights of man.

All the while, the Unitarians were claiming me as one of their own. Publications in both London and Boston wrote of me as a founder of the Unitarian movement in India. There was never any question that I was a Unitarian in believing in the essential and exclusive oneness of the Creative Force of the Universe. Furthermore, as I had indicated in my writings, I was an admirer of the ethical precepts of the Jesus of the Gospels. But at no time did I ever indicate a willingness to accept the historical or cultural accoutrements which had attached themselves to Christianity over the centuries.

It seemed to me to be a very natural development for the Hindu adherents of the Calcutta Unitarian Society to choose in 1828 to declare their independence from British-style Christian Unitarianism and establish the Brahmo Somaj, a specifically Hindu expression of the same religious quest.

William Adam was devastated by this development. Shortly afterwards he left India and ultimately renounced the ministry.

A tragic irony, it seems to me, is the fact that we were at least a century and a half ahead of our times. As much of Unitarian Universalism has evolved in your day, the early 21st century, into a much less Christian and much more inclusive search for eternal truth, the idea of a Hindu Unitarian manifestation would hardly raise an eyebrow.

Islamic, Buddhist, Taoist, Christian, Hindu, Pantheist and many other diverse traditions have easily been enveloped in the loving embrace of this rational spiritual community. If it had only been that way in my day!

Good Morning. I am

MARY CARPENTER

I was the oldest of the six children of Dr. and Mrs. Lant Carpenter. Father was a well-known Unitarian minister and educator and my mother was equally as skilled as a teacher. I was born in 1807 in Exeter, Devon but grew to maturity in Bristol after father settled in Lewin's Mead Chapel in that city.

Like many other Unitarian ministers of that era, Father ran a school primarily for the sons of the wealthy and professional class. Even though such education was unusual for girls I was permitted to attend classes with the boys. At a very early age I even began to teach classes of my own.

When I was once asked to summarize my childhood, I answered: "I learned early how to be useful."

When I was old enough I worked as a governess. Then at the age of 22 I opened a school of my own. The Chapel in Bristol was located quite near the most blighted slums of the city, and seeing children living in such squalor day after day, year after year, compelled me to forsake schooling for the well-to-do and open what was called a "ragged school." That was in 1846.

My school had special rules of its own. It was based on mutual confidence and trust between pupils and teachers. There was no corporal punishment. Neither was any child ever held up to ridicule. Teachers were required to become acquainted with the child's home environment. And, in addition to formal training there were regularly scheduled field trips to other places of interest and personal enrichment.

I discovered that many children lacked the discipline to function in such an atmosphere, but knew that we could not forsake them to their delinquency. Thus, I established the Red Lodge Reform School for the unruly. Based on our observations there I published two books: *Reformatory Schools for the Children of the Perishing and Dangerous Classes* in 1851, and two years later, *Juvenile Delinquents, their Condition and Treatment.* My findings and recommendations were accepted by the British Parliament which incorporated them into the Juvenile Offenders Act of 1854.

In addition, I made certain that our schools provided after-care, maintaining contact with our students and assisting them in finding constructive employment.

In subsequent years I was successful in convincing government to adopt many of these ideas into the Industrial Act of 1857 and amendments in succeeding sessions. These included the establishment of day-feeding industrial schools of which I was most proud. As word of our important reforms spread I was invited to travel to America, Canada and France to study and consult on delinquency and prison concerns.

But the crowning achievement of my life came much later in the establishment of schools for the education of women and girls in India. Let me provide some background on this matter.

In 1830, when I was in my early 20's, the renowned Indian scholar, Raja Ram Mohan Roy, visited our home at the invitation of my father. He was the intellectual and spiritual leader of a religious renaissance in his native land. From his pulpit, Father referred to our esteemed guest as "the day-star of Unitarianism which has arisen in the East." In his sermon that morning he spoke of the inter-connectedness of the recently deceased Wilberforce's liberation of African slaves and an equally great liberation of other people of color foretold in the life of Ram Mohan.

The opportunity to get to know, converse at length and in depth, and share the great spirit of this incredible man, made an impression on me that never left me for an hour for the remainder of my life.

Another source of inspiration for me was Joseph Tuckerman, the beloved Unitarian minister from Boston. He had come to England in order that he, also, might meet Ram Mohan. While he was in Bristol he became ill, and required an extended period of recovery. But even when he should have been convalescing he demanded that I show him around the slums of our city. When one ragged boy dashed across our path, Dr. Tuckerman said: "That boy should be followed home and looked after." His words sank into my mind with the painful feeling of a duty that was being neglected. Much of what I attempted to do for boys and girls like that was the result of what he said that day.

In an even deeper sense, Raja Ram Mohan, sent me to India nearly four decades after his death. I made the first of four visits in 1866. This trip was largely for observation of the situation of female education. What I learned I took back to England with me the next year as I began to build a base for specific actions.

Education, I discovered, was a monopoly of the missionaries. Government had little commitment in this regard. This meant that many Hindu and Muslim youth were simply excluded. The situation for boys was less than adequate and for girls almost non-existent. I returned to India in 1868 with a commitment from the British government to do more for the 200 million subjects of our beloved Queen. Plans were laid on this trip for the establishment of normal schools for women and girls. I was convinced there would never be adequate education for girls unless we were able to train a significant corps of female teachers.

This trip led to the publication of *Six Months in India*, which was read with interest by Queen Victoria herself. She invited me to the palace to discuss my ideas. I left that meeting with a firm commitment from Her Majesty to support my efforts.

Time does not permit a full recitation of our accomplishments in the following years. Let me simply state that Normal Schools were established in Madras, Poona, Ahmadabad and Hyderabad. Many believe that the course of Indian history was transformed by these institutions.

My Unitarian faith was very important to me, but I was always careful not to proselytize in the aggressive style of the missionaries. Still I always knew that if "female education" was to spread and flourish, it was vital that schools be free of any connection with the Christian religion. That represented too much the continuing spirit of colonialism.

I was 60 years old before I first visited that wonderful land, but it dominated my life. Isn't it ironic that a Victorian spinster could exert such influence in a country where unmarried women counted for so little.

Yet, in India I was called "Mother." It was certainly with motherly concern that I fought so tenaciously for the uneducated girls, the factory children, and the prisoners.

Back in Bristol, in 1877, I died and was buried in Arnos Vale near the grave of the noble Raja who had inspired me so many years before.

Good Morning. I am

MARGARET BARR

I spent 34 years working among the Khasi people in India, but I was never a missionary! Let's get that straight right at the beginning. I went to India from my native England with the intent of identifying myself as completely as possible with the people of India and to become one with them in every way. I had no wish for them to think of me as in any way, through either Government or Missions, identified with the British in India, save by the accident of my birth which had made me British.

That was not possible, of course. My physical appearance clearly said that I was a white person from the Western world. No matter what my intentions the way I looked shouted "Imperialist" and "Evangelist" to the indigenous population.

But let's go back to the beginning. I was born in the final year of the 19th century into a theologically conservative Methodist family. In my adolescent years I had many questions but was only told that I must put my doubts aside, and trust and obey.

As soon as I got to Girton College at Cambridge I began to explore other options. When I attended my first Unitarian service I felt like some watcher of the skies when a new planet swims into his ken. I knew at once that I had come home and the quest for a religious affiliation able to satisfy me intellectually, emotionally and spiritually was ended.

At age 22 I began my studies to become a Unitarian minister. I might have spent my life in a settled ministry in England but for two important influences. The first was my sister who had gone to India as a Methodist missionary and had found a teaching position as a village worker under Mahatma Gandhi. She sensitized me to the plight of the Indian nationals in their own country under the domination of Great Britain.

Then at a General Assembly of our churches I learned of an indigenous Unitarian movement in the Khasi Hills of Assam, India which had been established a half century earlier by Hajom Kissor Singh.

Ever since I had heard of Gandhi I had been conscious of a vague but steadily deepening conviction that somehow my life work was to be bound up with his. And when I heard of Hajom Kissor Singh and his work in the Khasi Hills, I knew with a deeper certainty that my life work would be tied to his. These two, together, carried the divine command which took me to India.

The British General Assembly turned down my request to be commissioned to go to India. Their refusal was not because I lacked qualifications, but because I was a single woman. Their approval was to be contingent upon me finding a suitable female companion.

I arranged for a teaching position in Calcutta on my own. I resigned my ministry in Rotherham, and in October 1933, at the age of 34, set sail to pursue my dream.

Shortly after my arrival I met with Gandhi who advised me to find some constructive work to do. I asked if that meant village work, and he responded: "What else is worth doing in comparison with serving those who need you most?"

It was necessary, however, for me to remain in Calcutta, for a period of two years. During that time I taught in a liberal state school, developed a curriculum on world religions and published a book, *The Great Unity: A New Approach to World Religions*.

The Unitarian leaders in London then relented and agreed to support me while I spent a year in the Khasi Hills seeing what I could do. That one year extended itself into three decades. I made periodic trips back to England to report on my activities and to raise funds for the work. But these trips were always of short duration and I hurried back to my true home. The only exception to this were the years of 1943-44 when England was under heavy bombardment and threatened invasion. I felt it was necessary for me to be there at that time. But as soon as that siege was over I returned to my beloved Khasi Hills and the people of the nineteen congregations scattered among the remote villages.

My primary work was with Gandhi's "Basic Education," which was an educational process designed to start rural people on the path toward literacy and self-sufficiency. I dedicated the last two decades of my working life to this endeavor.

I took eight or ten children at a time who lived with me as a family. When they had completed the primary level, we faced a great problem. The district had no middle or high schools which they could attend. So, for those who wished to continue I made a deal. If they would help instruct the next group of incoming children I would tutor them for the intermediate and high school examinations. Everyone of these young people passed the state level exams, many with honors.

These children were my salvation, each individuality to be respected, developed and loved. I will admit that my life in India often lacked intellectual and spiritual companionship, but I was never lonely. There were always the children with whom I could dance or play, sing or read.

Everything I attempted was founded on the conviction that education was the essential ingredient to bringing dignity and self-sufficiency to the people of the villages. Ever since becoming a Unitarian at Cambridge I knew that my work was not to seek to influence others to join my church, but to do something more. It was to be a bridge-builder and to find fellowship with others in the environment in which the spirit could take wings and life could be lived in a manner worthy of its divine origin.

We all have so much to learn from others, if we would only keep ourselves open to new truths and insights. I frequently advised friends in England to read the Bhagavad Gita if they wanted to understand the teachings of Jesus, particularly the Sermon on the Mount. I recommend it to you, as well.

What matters, after all, is not that we should all think alike—heaven forbid!—but that having experienced God in our own way, we should see to it that the fruits of experience are to be seen in our lives and that we should be ready to admit that other people's paths to God, though different from our own, may be equally effective.

Good Morning. I am

THOMAS FYSHE PALMER

I was born to a Bedfordshire, England landowner at the midpoint of the 18th century. I was educated at Eton and then studied for the Anglican ministry at Queens College, Cambridge.

These were years of political ferment, immediately preceding the revolutions in both the American colonies and in France. It was inevitable that I was influenced by these dramatic expressions of the desire for human liberation.

After graduation I became a curate at Leatherhead in Surrey, but felt an emptiness and lack of direction in my life. Then I discovered the writings of Joseph Priestley, the radical Unitarian. The more I learned of his theological opinions the more dissatisfied I became with the doctrines of the Church of England. I had been vaguely aware of these stirrings of discontent for quite some time, but discerned no feasible alternative until I came under the tutelage of Priestley.

This led me to renounce my Anglican vows and move to Montrose in Scotland where a small group of Unitarians had established a chapel. For the next several years I not only provided leadership to this gathering but also traveled extensively in Scotland helping to form other Unitarian groups.

My active role in the campaign for religious toleration in Scotland led directly into greater involvement in the growing secular movement for political and Parliamentary reform.

In 1892, a group of English political leaders, headed by Lord John Russell, established the Friends of the People to work for reform in England. I followed by organizing a similar Friends of Liberty in Dundee. We were a collection of weavers, shoemakers, blacksmiths and other working men who were denied participation in the political arena.

In Scotland, at that time, only 1 person out of every 250 was permitted to vote. We read Thomas Paine's treatise on The Rights of Man and heard echoes of the French cries of Liberty, Equality, Fraternity. We could not sit idly by without rising up to struggle for ourselves and our countrymen.

A year later, in 1793, I was arrested and charged with sedition for having written a pamphlet, entitled *Dundee Address to the Friends of Liberty*, which was highly critical of the British government. It was claimed that I was guilty of "writing or printing seditious or inflammatory writing, calculated to produce a spirit of discontent in the minds of the people against the present happy constitution and government of this country, and to rouse them to acts of outrage and violence."

Now, while I, indeed, did wish to produce a spirit of discontent in the minds of the people, the truth is that I did not write that particular pamphlet. It was composed by an unlettered weaver named George Mealmaker who was a member of our society. The authorities refused to believe that a man of the working class was capable of such incisive thinking and erudite expression, even though he appeared in court at my trial and claimed authorship for himself.

I had, however, as the government claimed, distributed this pamphlet widely as I traveled throughout Scotland campaigning for reform. The prosecution called me "the most determined rebel in Scotland." That was an epithet I wore with pride, even though I knew in my heart, that such an honor should be shared with any number of others of my comrades.

Along with three others from the Friends of Liberty, I was sentenced to seven years of what was called "transportation." That simply meant exile to the newly formed colony of Australia.

A small group of just men in the British House of Commons named us the *Scottish Martyrs*, and launched a campaign to overturn the conviction, but their efforts were in vain.

In May in the year 1794 the ship carrying me to exile left Portsmouth for the 13,000 mile voyage to Botany Bay in New South Wales. I remained a political prisoner during my years in that place. I was not permitted to preach or to organize, but was allowed to engage in commerce and supported myself by transporting goods to Norfolk Island.

My seven year sentence was completed in 1801 and I chose to return to my homeland. Our ship encountered a terrible storm and was forced to seek safe harbor. Our only port of refuge was on the island of Guam which was under the control of the Spanish who took the crew and all passengers prisoners. While held as a prisoner of war I contracted dysentery and died in January 1802.

The essence of my life can be best expressed, I believe, through words I spoke at my trial for treason. At that time I said: "My life has been employed in the dissemination of what I conceived to be religious and moral truths. My friends know with what ardor I have done this, at the sacrifice of all my worldly interests. But during the late great political discussions, it was naturally impossible, in a man of my sanguine disposition to remain an unconcerned bystander."

That is how I wish to be remembered. If, however, you visit Waterloo Place in Edinburgh, you may observe a monument erected in honor of the Scottish Martyrs. Inscribed on it are words of our compatriot Thomas Muir, who spoke for us all when he said: "I have devoted myself to the cause of the people. It is a good cause. It shall ultimately prevail. It shall finally triumph."

Good Morning. I am

CATHERINE HELEN SPENCE

My likeness now appears on the five dollar note of Australia, but my first sight of this country with which I am so closely associated caused me to break down in tears.

I had been born in the hill country of Scotland on October 31 in the year 1825. It was there I spent my childhood years and studied at the feet of my beloved teacher Sarah Phinn at St. Mary's School. That may sound like a Catholic institution, but I assure you it was quite sufficiently Protestant. Scotch Presbyterian to be exact. Calvinist to the core.

Then our family emigrated to the newly founded colony of South Australia. We arrived there on my fourteenth birthday. I looked about at the arid landscape, thought of the lush greenery of Scotland, and in spite of the dignity of my just attained 14 years, sat down on a bench and had a good cry.

Father found a position as Town Clerk in Adelaide and worked with a Municipal Council elected by the radical process of proportional representation. He explained to me how this unique concept greatly increased the voices of minorities. I adopted the idea as my own, and for the next half century became our nation's leading advocate of this form of democratic suffrage. Many have credited me with leading the fight for Women's Suffrage in Australia, and while I certainly crusaded for giving women the right to vote, I was more concerned with the idea of proportional representation. Effective Voting, it was called.

But this gets me ahead of my story. After we settled in Adelaide, I took employment as a governess of small children. Then, when I was 17, my sister Mary and I organized a school. While teaching I also wrote articles for a newspaper my brother was publishing. My articles, however, always appeared under his name as it was considered unseemly for a woman to appear in print.

Two years later I wrote a series of articles supporting John Stuart Mills' arguments in favor of ballot reform. This time the publisher agreed to append my initials, if not my name, to my writing.

As I mentioned before, I was raised in the Calvinistic tradition. It was a dour and depressing faith. On reaching maturity, I knew I could not agree with doctrines such as predestination and the total depravity of man. But I had nothing to put in the place of that which I rejected and continued as if living under a cloud.

Then I discovered Unitarianism. The cloud was lifted from my universe. I became the most cheerful person you could ever know, and remained so throughout my entire life. I never considered the ministry as a vocation, but I did preach at least one hundred times at the Unitarian Churches in various Australian cities.

I did lots of public speaking over the years. There is no way the number of speeches and lectures could be counted. All of that happened after I had reached the age of 40. As a matter of fact, my first lecture was on my impressions of England delivered to the South Australian Institute in 1866. The amazing thing is that I was not even in attendance when it happened. Women did not speak in public in those days, and my words were read by a man in my absence!

My primary profession was as a journalist and a writer, but my deep interest in other causes demanded a goodly proportion of my time.

I helped organize the State Children's Council in 1871 which moved parentless and neglected children out of asylums and into private homes.

I worked with other dedicated women in developing Children's Courts, a movement begun in South Australia. My book on our experiences in this venture led to the adoption of a similar system in England in 1907.

I was the first woman appointed to a School Board in Australia. The first woman member of a Hospital Committee. A founding member of the Criminological Society which worked for prison reform. And, founder of the National Council of Women in South Australia. And, later, the first president of the Women's Non-Party Political Association.

All the while I was primarily campaigning for Effective Election reform. That was the true passion of my life. I was considered a weak-kneed sister by those who worked exclusively for woman suffrage, although I was as much convinced as they that I was entitled to a vote . . . and hoped I might be able to exercise it before I was too feeble to hobble to the poll.

I always encouraged women to take up the challenge of the work to reform. I recognized that the home is the center of woman's sphere—as it should be—but in too many cases that has been permitted to be its limitation. The larger social life has been ignored, and women have failed to have the influence on public life of which they are capable.

I have hardly mentioned the many books I had published. But if you are interested in them, you can find them on my Home Page of your incredible invention called the Internet. My, oh my, what a wonder!

Oh yes, I also constructed Crosswords and Acrostics for the newspapers. One book of Charades and Double Acrostics was published and sold to raise funds for a home for people with incurable diseases.

I lived to the glorious age of 85, ten years into the 20th century.

But I consider the 19th to have been the most wonderful century. What a challenging and exciting time to have lived.

All through my life I tried to live up to the best that was in me. I never forgot what my beloved teacher, Sarah Phin, wrote to me just before we left Scotland. She called me the ornament of her school, her best girl and best scholar. She said I should undertake useful causes. She said I was certain to succeed and would never need to be afraid. I always tried to live up to her confidence in me.

I am pleased with all the public accolades that have been heaped on me by the women and men of Australia. But most of all I hope to be remembered as one who never swerved in her efforts to do her duty to herself and her fellow citizens.

Good Morning. I am

JOHN CRAWFORD WOODS

In Adelaide in the colony of South Australia in the autumn of 1854, a small group of men met in the law offices of Francis Clark & Sons and agreed to establish the Unitarian Christian Church. All of the founders had been Unitarians in England before emigrating to their new home.

The following September I arrived in Adelaide from my native Ireland to assume responsibilities as their minister. Shortly thereafter we held our first publicly announced service in Green Land's Exchange. It was attended by a respectable and deeply attentive congregation of nearly 200 persons. Most were there, probably, out of curiosity and a desire to hear more about strange doctrines that were generally considered to be heresy.

Among those in attendance at that first service was Catherine Helen Spence. I did not know it at the time, but she later confided to some close friends that she was "greatly impressed," and intended to listen to my preaching for three months. After that period she would decide whether to cast her lot with us. She was true to her word and did not miss a service, either Sunday morning or evening, for that prescribed period.

During that time I preached a series of sermons describing, as best I could, my interpretation of basic Unitarian approaches to religious faith and life. I lectured on "Jesus Christ, Son of God, not God the Son." I did not go as far as some of my contemporaries in Britain or the United States in teaching that Jesus was only a man. A just man. A holy man. Worthy of emulation. But only a man. This point of view was consistent with the prevailing position of the majority of the congregation which voted down several attempts to have the term Christian erased from our institutional name.

I presented to my listeners a portrait of the deity that was diametrically opposite to that portrayed by the Presbyterian Church of Scotland from which most of them had emerged. Rather than a God of oppressive retribution who pre-determined the destiny of mankind, and foreordained most of them to eternal damnation, I spoke of a deity that was the embodiment of justice and benevolence. God is not, I said, like a man with a liability to change his mind and repent of what he had done, with personal favorites and personal foes, but one who is infinitely wise and infinitely good, a God of love.

A third major theme in that introductory series of sermons was that the Unitarian way of religion was to strive to live in accordance with the creator's law, the laws of nature. We should engage our intellects in a search for truth. We should submit all things to the test of reason. We should be unhampered by traditional dogma and be unrestrained in our questioning of all authority—whether ecclesiastical or Biblical. Reason and knowledge are the keynotes of our way.

Happily, this way of looking at life struck a responsive chord in the mind and soul of Miss Spence, and she joined us and became a life-long Unitarian. She declared that a dark cloud—the residual of her Calvinistic upbringing—was lifted, that "her confused conscience was made clear and straight, her rebellious heart made submissive and contented." She wrote my wife, many years later, "I have been a very cheerful person ever since, more comfortable to my friends, and more serviceable to the world."

If I accomplished nothing else on this earth, those first sermons I preached in Adelaide, which led to Catherine Spence's conversion to Unitarianism made my life worthwhile.

Of course, I believe there were other things as well. I spent nearly half a century with that congregation, and together we accomplished many wonderful things. There were so many interesting and talented people in our fellowship that we had an

150

impact on the life of Australia far beyond our small numbers in the total population.

Like Unitarians everywhere I believe, and our people believed, there is something better for a man than to be concerned for his own personal salvation. I challenged people to catch the spirit of that which I call Enthusiasm for Humanity.

As a religious institution we did not seek to change society, but we did urge our members to do so in their secular pursuits. Our mission, as we understood it, was to change people so that they could change the world.

John Baker, one of the original founders, was a progressive member of South Australia's first elected Legislature. He was a crusader for education. He berated parents who took their children out of school and put them to work. "In this colony," he said, "where every man can educate his children, there can be no excuse for the prevalence of ignorance."

Arthur Hardy, another of the founders, developed an institute for the education of workers in his quarry.

Howard Clark taught at the Adelaide Educational Institute and presided at the founding of the South Australia Philosophical Society.

Catherine Helen Spence has already related to you many of the important causes she tirelessly supported. She was also in the forefront of efforts to achieve equality for women within our congregation.

Other women of that era were exhorting their sisters to gladly accept their secondary estate of supposed inferiority to men.

The women of the Adelaide Unitarian Church would have none of that. They taught in our Sunday School. They spoke from our pulpit. They established the Female Refuge and raised funds for the Children's Hospital. Annie Martin ran a school which was the model for progressive education and Edith Cook became headmistress of South Australia's Advanced School for Girls.

All in all, I have no doubt that the Unitarian Church of Adelaide made a difference, and I am grateful for having had the opportunity to be a part of its early years.

Good Morning. I am

MARTHA TURNER

When I was appointed minister of the Melbourne Unitarian Church in 1874 I became the first woman minister of any denomination in Australia.

More astounding, perhaps, is the fact that I was most likely the first Unitarian woman minister in the entire British Empire. At least that is what Florence and Rosamund Hill, the English Unitarian reformers, said when they visited in 1875.

My elevation to that position came about in an uncommon way. Our congregation was established in 1853 by a group of prominent citizens, among whom was my brother Henry Gyles Turner. The original membership was restricted to men.

The role of women is indicated in minutes of our Church Committee in 1854. A motion read: "That the ladies of the Church willing to assist in making preparations for a tea party be requested to stay after the morning service. That the husbands of such ladies be appointed to manage the business relative to the tea party."

Gradually, agonizing step-by-step, we gained greater acceptance. First, we were accepted as members with a vote in congregational elections. Then, in 1871 women were permitted to stand for office, though it was another two decades before any chose to do so.

But back to my story. I first came to Australia in 1870 from my native England. It was intended to be a relatively short visit with my brother Henry, but I was so enamored by the country, I decided to make it my permanent place of residence.

In my earlier years I had received a far better than usual education for a girl of that time. My parents had arranged for me to attend a secondary school in Dijon, France which emphasized academic pursuits not often available to members of my sex.

The Unitarian minister, Henry Higginson, died the same year I arrived in Melbourne and the church was unable to find a suitable replacement. For three years they functioned with a series of lay preachers. One of these was my brother, Henry. Quite often he prevailed upon me to write the sermons which he then read as his own.

On occasions when he was ill-disposed I delivered the message myself. When it became known in the congregation that I had been the author of his sermons, I was asked to assume the responsibilities of preparation and delivery of sermons on a regular basis. Many members, including my dear friend Catherine Spence said I did a better job than any of the men, and that led to my appointment as the regular minister.

I did not assume that responsibility without great fear and trepidation. I worried that the natural conservative instinct of women would lead the ladies of the congregation to discountenance or forsake me. That anxiety was unfounded as the women surrounded me with unstinting support.

But, nonetheless, being a product of my time and steeped in the traditional role of women I was concerned whether or not my appointment was in accord with the proper fitness of things.

It was common in those days for newspapers to report Sunday services at a variety of churches, often reproducing the text of sermons in their entirety. It took some time before the papers reported anything about the Unitarian services other than my manner of dress and whether I exhibited any "obtrusive womanhood . . . to urge the idea of sex and its special characteristics on your attention."

But gradually, as is almost always the case, things began to change and I was accepted as a person with a mission to fulfill and not simply as a curiosity. The novelty wore off and we became a church again instead of a carnival side-show.

Pockets of opposition remained in the congregation among some who felt that the gender of the minister was an obstacle to growth. They maintained that the Church Committee should keep looking "for a suitable gentleman."

Five years after I assumed my ministerial duties, at the age of 39, I married a banker by the name of John Webster. My brother, Henry Gyles Turner, advised me to tender my resignation. It was his feeling that it was not proper for a married woman to hold such a position. This was very much in keeping with the Victorian idea that while unmarried women might work as governesses it was a violation of propriety for a woman of the middle class to be gainfully employed.

I accepted his advise and offered my resignation. Much to my surprise and pleasure, the Committee unanimously refused the offer and I continued in my clerical role for another five years.

My ministry was not particularly noteworthy in many respects. I was never a firebrand social reformer like many other Unitarian clergy who preceded and followed me in the Melbourne church. I was a strong supporter of woman suffrage, but never a crusader in that regard.

My theology was probably a little more conservative than that espoused by others. I had grown up in a more evangelical religious environment. Unitarianism was not my birthright or cradle-faith. I came to it later in life. I certainly preached a liberal gospel, but rejected the extreme humanistic interpretation of Jesus which many others had adopted.

My preaching style was academic and devoid of any theatrics or exaggerated enthusiasm. This was my nature. At all times I attempted to be myself, and nothing other than myself.

After ten years the congregation found that "suitable gentleman," Reverend George Walters, to replace me. My husband and I visited Europe and England. There I was greeted enthusiastically and was invited to preach in a goodly number of Unitarian Chapels.

We then returned to Melbourne where I continued to offer volunteer services to the congregation until my death at the age of 76.

Good Morning. I am

WILLIAM BOTTOMLEY

For 23 years, from 1926 to 1949, I was the minister of the Melbourne Unitarian Church. The year after I assumed the responsibilities of that pulpit the Melbourne Church celebrated its 75th anniversary. On that occasion I said: "This Unitarian Church is essentially a Modernist Christian Church. It is free to advance to new positions, and to change its views about God and the universe, as the new knowledge advances."

Such a pronouncement may sound quaint and old-fashioned to Unitarians in the 21st century, but I assure you it situated us on the more radical wing of the British Unitarianism of that day.

I was born in Yorkshire, England in 1882. My mother died when I was an infant and I lost my father when I was only sixteen. I never fully recovered from that loss throughout my entire lifetime. Father was a Wesleyan minister and I always intended to follow his example. In fact, I preached my first sermon only one year after his death.

Methodism and the Labor Movement were the two great unifying forces in my life. I became a lay preacher and a wool clerk, working during the day and studying at night. My reading led me more and more to view Jesus not as the Son of God, but as the model for man.

By the time I became acquainted with Unitarian minister Rev. John Ellis, I had already become a Unitarian without even knowing it. Ellis encouraged me to do some lay preaching for the Unitarian church and also arranged for me to be paid as an agent for the Independent Labour Party. This combination was a perfect fit for me at that stage in my life. I was a Socialist, though not a Marxist. I found in my newly acquired religious ideas a basis for my political views. The attraction of Jesus was in his humanity. I found in the words of Jesus the essence of a socialist philosophy.

Then the Great War, what you now call World War I, intervened and I served in the British army. But when it was ended I entered the Unitarian ministry on a full-time basis. I served congregations in Taunton and Yeovil where I spoke strongly in behalf of the poor, but sought to remain aloof from partisan politics.

When emigrating to Australia to accept the pulpit in Melbourne, I inherited a legacy of socially activist ministers. The issues I confronted in Australia were not the dire poverty of the English underclass, but more related to human rights and political reform.

I mustn't speak at length about all the issues I was involved in over a quarter of a century. But they pretty well covered the waterfront; from birth control, divorce law reform, prostitution, housing, employment, immigration reform, and peace. Needless to say, in most instances my positions were quite different from those espoused by the clergy of the orthodox churches.

In 1937, only eleven days before a federal election, I was approached by an acquaintance asking me to stand as a candidate for Parliament. He even offered to pay all my expenses. With less than two weeks to campaign I garnered nearly 20% of the votes against a future Prime Minister, Harold Holt. I ran, proudly, as an advocate for "Social Credit" as a way to lift the nation out of the economic depression.

Two years later I received considerable publicity when I offered to change places for a few days with Prime Minister Robert Menzies to give him "the opportunity to meet men without jobs, without homes, without sustenance, who were dependent on six-pences and shillings given to them in the streets." The honorable Mr. Menzies did not accept my offer.

During these years the awful shadow of fascism was spreading over the world. I was an outspoken opponent of Nazism and worked diligently to get Australia to open its doors to Jews and other refugees. My close working relationship with Rabbi Sanger on that matter was most enriching.

My experiences in the first World War deeply influenced my thinking about another coming conflict. I became an active member of the Australian Pacifist Movement and preached numerous sermons on the subject. Not all of the members of our church agreed with me on this, and some left our fellowship. But many others joined us because of our stand against war. Many others who disagreed with my position remained loyal to the church despite holding contrary opinions. Bless them for that!

Government agents, Security Service officials, regularly attended our services during these years to keep watch on me. They always looked decidedly uncomfortable, I observed, during our singing of hymns and offering up prayers for peace.

All of this, I believed, was in harmony with the religious faith we proclaimed. My Jesus, and the Jesus of most of our congregation, I believe, was not a savior who died for the sins of mankind, but "Jesus the Militant, the revolutionary, the humanitarian, the ethical ideal for modern times."

On a nationwide radio broadcast I argued against an artificial separation of the religious and non-religious areas of life. I argued that the so-called non-religious areas were where religion had its greatest responsibility. When I saw 16,000 children in Melbourne ill-housed and under-fed everyday, I did not need any special religious insight to know what God's will was in that matter.

Some folks told me that as I got older I seemed to get more mellow. I don't know whether that is true or not. I do know that I never stopped my lifelong search for new truth and new avenues of service to my fellowman. I know I never wavered in my devotion to liberalism and the social gospel. Perhaps my later emphasis on the more personal aspects of the quest for meaning in life was nothing other than a vindication of my earlier activism.

God Morgen. Jeg er

KRISTOFER JANSON

Born into a wealthy and aristocratic family in Bergen, Norway, in the year 1841, others predicted that I was destined to become either a political leader or the Bishop of the established Lutheran Church.

To the contrary, I became a poet, an author, the founding minister of Unitarian churches in three different countries, and the champion of the "peasant language" movement in my native land.

It is difficult to describe when and how I turned away from my privileged heritage and was seized by idealism and democracy. As a boy I amused my parents and their aristocratic friends by reciting poems of my own creation which ridiculed the peasant class and their simple speech.

Yet, by the time I had reached the University of Oslo I delivered my Freshman Oration in the very dialect I had earlier lampooned. Such audacity on my part was shocking both to my elders and my peers. It did not, however, keep me from graduating with highest honors and a degree in theology.

After graduation I joined two friends in establishing a high school for peasants in the hills of central Norway. One of my colleagues in this venture was Bjornstjerne Bjornson, the recipient of the 1903 Nobel Prize for Literature. The other, the noted educator Kristofer Bruun. We were all, in our own ways, writers. We each produced many of our finest works during those years together at our school.

My own work, which paled in comparison to that of Bjornson, ranged from historical narratives, to poems, dramas, fairy tales, hymns and novels.

In 1879 I traveled to America for a lecture tour at the invitation of the Norwegian immigrant communities which had been established in Minnesota and Wisconsin. These months were a major turning point in my life. I had gone to America to lecture to peasant-farmers in their own vernacular on social topics and Norse folk tales which helped them feel less far removed from home. As long as I stuck to such non-controversial themes I was lauded and lionized.

But I had long harbored nearly-hidden antagonism against the ruling church and its authoritarian and dogmatic ways. I found these anti-democratic tendencies magnified in the American immigrant communities. The pastors were dictators, demanding unquestioned allegiance to their narrow views. I was scandalized by the ways they attempted to discourage these sons and daughters of the Vikings from participation in the larger American culture.

Also, during this trip, I had become acquainted with the writings of Channing, Theodore Parker, James Freeman Clarke, and other Unitarian leaders. I had met with contemporary Unitarian ministers such as Jenkin Lloyd Jones and J. T. Sutherland. I found in them the alternative to dogmatism for which I had long been searching.

I was emboldened to begin to speak openly of my opposition to the Norwegian Lutheran Church. I challenged its rigid fundamentalism, its opposition to public schools, its attempts to keep parishioners from inclusion in the larger democratic social order.

The press, in both American and Norway, suddenly turned against me with a vengeance. No longer hailed a hero, I was now denounced as the worst of scoundrels.

When the lecture tour was over I returned home. I then discovered it was a very dangerous thing in Norway to express doubts about the Lutheran Creed, and the verbal inspiration and infallibility of the Bible. The ecclesiastic hierarchy could not cause you to be crucified, burned at the stake, or sent to Siberia or some Devil's Island in the sea, but it could effectively prevent you from earning a living. I was forbidden from returning to my teaching position at the school.

Not long after I received an invitation from the head of the Scandinavian studies program at the University of Wisconsin to return to America as a Unitarian missionary to the farmer-folk of the old Northland.

In the following twelve years I established congregations in Minneapolis, St. Paul, and three other smaller communities. In addition, I served as part time minister of the Nora Church in Madelia, Minnesota. Nora—named for the sister countries of Norway, Sweden and Denmark—had been founded by a small group of independent-minded farmers in 1881. They had never before heard of Unitarianism, but found my messages to their liking.

Our first building there was destroyed by a tornado shortly before it was completed. The neighboring Lutherans said this was evidence of the judgment of God. The fact that their own building had been lifted off its foundation by the same wind went unmentioned.

You will find it hard to believe the difficulties faced by these liberal pioneers. They were condemned for their apostasy and shunned by their neighbors. Many who were blood relatives or who had come from the same Norwegian villages refused to ever again speak to those who took fellowship with our congregations.

In 1893, for a variety of personal reasons, I returned to Christiania, which you know today as Oslo. There I established the first Unitarian congregation in any of the Scandinavian countries. Among my parishioners was Nina Grieg, wife of the composer Edvard Grieg. Nina was an important person in the establishment of the Unitarian Church in Copenhagen at a later time. She was a member of the Christiania congregation. Her husband never joined but regularly attended our services, and was an outspoken critic of the State Church. The same was true of the two great literary figures, my friends, Henrik Ibsen and Bjorn Bjornson.

In addition, I spent some time in Aarhus, Denmark's second largest city, and organized a congregation there. I both preached and lectured on numerous occasions for the church in Copenhagen, so I feel very close to the development of Unitarianism there as well as in Norway.

It is fair to say that my religion was Unitarianism with a Christian orientation. But I remained open to the intimations of truth inherent in all the great religions of the world. Even in my years of high school teaching I told my students that the Bible stories they thought beautiful would be just as beautiful if told by Buddha, or Mohammed, or Zoroaster. If my beliefs veered in any direction is was probably toward Buddhism.

My second wife was a great believer in Spiritualism, and many thought she was an undue influence on me in this regard. I counseled against the "side-show" expressions of this, such as attempts to make contact with the dead. I did, however, investigate the possibility of receiving guidance from higher evolved beings.

There are many other things I would like to share with you, but I fear I have overstayed my assigned time. Let me summarize my Credo with some lines I wrote during one period of raging conflict:

> Battle for freedom to do what is good;
> Fight against all that is brutal and rude;
> Conquer your foe by the power of love;
> God be your guide wherever you rove.

164

God Morgen. Jeg er

NINA GRIEG

Even though I was a concert singer and pianist of considerable note in my own right, you will most likely recognize me as the wife of the immortal Norwegian composer, Edvard Grieg.

I was born in Norway in 1845. My father was Norwegian. My mother was the famous Danish actress, Madame Werleigh. When I was quite young we moved to Copenhagen where I remained until my marriage.

Edvard and I were cousins. Our mothers were sisters. I recall our first meeting, when we were both young children, at our grandfather's summer home outside of Bergen. We argued about who would get to use the swing which grandfather had strung up on the branch of a tree in his orchard. I claimed I should be allowed to swing first because I was visiting from Denmark. We certainly did not know it at the time, but that difference of opinion was the beginning of a beautiful love story that continued through half a century.

We met again when I was 18 and he was 20, when Edvard came to Copenhagen to study under the famous Danish musician Niels Gade. Mother and her second husband, an actor and director of a prosperous theatrical company, took an instant liking to their young nephew. He was a frequent guest in our home and companion at cultural events we attended together.

Matters cooled between my parents and Edvard, however, when they detected that he and I were becoming increasingly fond of one another. The fact that we were cousins did not disturb them. Marriage between cousins was quite common in the Scandinavian countries. Their concern was that he was determined to pursue a career in music rather than joining his father's business back in Bergen. Mother was determined that I would marry a man of means, and not an idealistic, struggling, and probably impoverished musician. "He is nothing, has nothing, and writes music no one will ever listen to," she said.

Edvard and I took a secret vow that we would wait for one another, for however long it might take, until he had achieved sufficient recognition as a composer. Then when our families could no longer oppose our union for financial reasons, we would marry. He celebrated our promise by setting to music words written by Hans Christian Andersen, who was a family friend.

> O thou my only joy, my only pleasure
> Thou in whose being I alone can be,
> I love thee more that all the earth my treasure,
> I love thee now, and for Eternity.

Little did either of us imagine then that "our song," Edvard's *I Love Thee*, would become one of his most cherished creations and be sung all over the world to this very day.

Four years later, totally unexpected and unsolicited praise from Franz Lisz gave Edvard the recognition that brought sufficient financial stability to enable us to marry and settle in Christiania, Norway.

A major breakthrough in his career came shortly thereafter when Henrik Ibsen decided to turn his long poem *Peer Gynt* into a drama for the stage. He commissioned Edvard to write a musical score to accompany the production. The play received little attention, but Grieg's *Peer Gynt Suite* remains a classic.

But that is enough about this part of our lives. I was invited to share something of my religious odyssey. Actually I have been doing that. So much of my spiritual quest has been intermingled with the beauty of music, the miracle of human love, and the life-affirming glory of nature.

My husband and I shared an antipathy toward the narrow dogmatism of the Norwegian State Church, but he was far more outspoken in his criticism than I could ever have been. As a very young boy it had been suggested that he might grow up to be a clergyman. To the contrary, I doubt that anyone ever detested the clergy more than he. Once he said, "As for the clergy, I can't stomach them. They make me vomit, and I seem unable ever to free myself from the abominable fatty taste of them."

Edvard was truly a tender and loving man. Really he was. It is difficult to reconcile the harshness of his criticism of the Church with the gentle spirit of the man I lived with for so many years. The death of his father seemed to intensify these feelings. He made a complete break with traditional Christianity and distanced himself from all ideas of Original Sin, the divinity of Jesus, and the concept of eternal punishment. He cancelled his membership in the State Church which he called "that poisonous dinosaur, which other than its total impotence, owns nothing but a poisonous sting."

Had he not become, by this time, a national hero, I am sure there would have been public censure, perhaps retribution, for this kind of expression of apostasy.

Fortunately for both of us, on a subsequent visit to England, Edvard became acquainted with a Unitarian minister in Birmingham whom he recognized as one of "his own kind."

When Kristofer Janson organized a Unitarian Church in Christiania in 1893 we found a new home. Edvard never became an official member, as I did, but he was regular in his attendance and supported me in every way. One of the things that appealed to both of us was a form of pantheism, the discovery and experience of the Divine in nature. We shared a sense that "poor is the person who is not drawn and beguiled by the profound mystique of the Nature of Music and the Music of Nature." That was one reason we left instructions that we be buried in a cave at our

Norwegian estate Troldhaugen . . . . The abode of the Trolls.

After my husband's death in 1905 I returned to Copenhagen where I lived for an additional 30 years until my own death at age 90.

Upon returning to Denmark I immediately identified myself with the newly established Danish Unitarian Church, which was called the Free Church Society.

I contributed as liberally as I could to the construction of the beautiful building which houses the congregation in Copenhagen. My major contribution, I suppose, was a series of concerts which I gave to raise money for the purchase of a magnificent organ. I'm sure it was what Edvard would have wished me to do.

God Morgen. Jeg er

MARY B. WESTENHOLZ

Because my mother was also named Mary, I was known to my family and closest friends as Bess.

I was the fourth of six children in the family of the wealthy Danish shipowner Regnar Westenholz. Since I was the only one of the six children who did not marry and have children, I was most commonly known as Aunt Bess.

We were all Unitarians. Our maternal grandmother was the British Unitarian Emma Eliza Grut, with whom we often spent our vacations.

There was no Unitarian Church in Denmark, or anywhere else in the Scandinavian countries, during my childhood and early adult years. It was not until I reached my 40's that our Free Church Society was founded in Copenhagen. That was in 1900. I became a founding member and remained active for the remaining 47 years of my life.

I was selected Secretary when we first organized, and became Chairperson five years later. At that same time I assumed editorship of our Church paper. I remained in both of these positions until 1918 when my good friend Thorvald Kierkegaard became our minister.

My favorite niece was the famous Danish writer Karen Blixen. You may know her better as Isak Dinesen, author of *Winter Tales* and the autobiographical *Out of Africa*. The fact that Karen published under a pseudonym tells you a lot about the status of women at that time.

I did my best to make a Unitarian out of her, but to no avail. She was certainly sympathetic to our Free Church approach but said she found our services "too intellectual and downright boring." Like many other Danes who agreed with us in rejecting the dogmatism of the State Church, she resisted a commitment to any specific faith that would make her feel, in her own words, "boxed in."

In Denmark we all became Lutherans by birth. We were baptized into the State Church and could only get out through a lengthy and burdensome process of official resignation. So, even after our Free Church Society was established, I remained a member of the State Church. It was a fervent desire of mine, naive perhaps, but deeply held, that the official church could be liberalized over time to the place where it could accept those with dissenting views.

Our minister, Uffe Birkedal, taught that Unitarians had an obligation to assist the State Church in the moderation of its rigid theological positions. He and I sought repeatedly to negotiate these matters with the church leaders, but were never able to get any acceptable response.

For that reason, I applied for the right to vote in the election of members of the Governing Council on my local Lutheran Church. My vote was rejected because of my "deviant" religious views which were displayed by my membership in the Free Church Society. Even a generous monetary donation to the State Church was refused and redirected to the local School Board, which was probably a better use for it. I challenged my rejection in court. Ultimately our Supreme Court ruled that Unitarians were a completely separate faith since we did not accept the Trinity.

This decision did not come as a surprise, but it did both anger and sadden me. It also strengthened my determination to work for a Unitarian movement which rejected dogmatic intolerance and narrow-mindedness, and encouraged diversity of opinion as signs of spiritual vitality and growth.

I never considered myself a public figure. I preferred to stay behind the scenes and work in concert with others. But I did have a temper, and when I saw others acting in hurtful or unethical ways, I did not hesitate to stand up and protest.

Other than filing suit against the State Church, the matter that put me most in the public eye occurred in 1909. The Danish Parliament had gone through a political scandal over the fraudulent use of public funds. I got so disgusted with the way the politicians were bickering and back-stabbing that I could stand it no longer.

So, one day I marched down to the Parliament chambers while they were in session, took the bell away from the chairman, and rang the room to silence. Then I proceeded to preach a fire and brimstone sermon to those assembled men, letting them know in no uncertain terms that the women of Denmark were completely fed-up and disgusted with their lack of ethics and irresponsible behavior. I made a strong case for giving women the right to vote as the only way in which the sorry situation they had created could be rectified. I had lots of other things to say, but was forcibly removed by the police. The newspapers reported that I had been "escorted by Parliamentary ushers." Cartoonists delighted in reproducing the scene.

My scandalous and un-womanly actions were rewarded by a procession of Danish women who ceremoniously marched to my home to pay tribute to my actions on their behalf. Six years later we were granted the franchise.

I take great satisfaction in having been a part of significant social change in my beloved country, and in having been associated with the establishment of liberal religion there.

Unitarianism was late in coming to Denmark. More than two centuries earlier Unitarians being driven into exile from Eastern Europe had sought permission from the Danish King to emigrate here. After consultation with the Bishops of our State Church he refused their request. Many subsequently found refuge in Holland and England. Through my English grandmother, this liberal faith re-crossed the Channel and came to Denmark.

We were originally, as I have indicated, a very specifically Christian form of Unitarianism. As I concluded my nearly half-a-century of fellowship with this band of spiritual pilgrims the congregation was a hospitable gathering of liberal Christians, Humanists, Pantheists, Agnostics, Atheists and a whole range of other varieties of seekers. I am confident that is even more the case today.

God Morgen. Jeg er

UFFE BIRKEDAL

I was raised in the parsonage of the State Church of Denmark, and destined, almost from birth, to follow the footsteps of my father into the Lutheran ministry.

How then did I, at age 48, at the dawn of the 20th century, become the founding pastor of Denmark's first Unitarian congregation? The answer is the essence of my Credo.

I attended the seminary, and was ordained after the required six years of arduous study. This was followed by nearly two decades of service to the Church.

Those years were fulfilling and enjoyable in many ways, but frustrating in many others. As a student I had been greatly influenced by our famous Danish theologian and hymn writer N. F. S. Grundtvig. You may know him best of the composer of "A Mighty Fortress Is Our God," but I knew him as one who taught his students to pursue their own quest for truth and not accept Church teaching without rigorous questioning. He was, himself, an orthodox believer, but wanted others to exercise the same kind of intellectual discipline he had brought to his personal search for meaning.

My quest brought me into frequent conflict with the official Church. I proceeded in the belief that the fight for freedom of the church was the road to the real truth of Christianity. This meant that I often challenged prevailing dogma much to the displeasure of my superiors.

I was also an ardent supporter of peace. On one occasion my public criticism of the Danish Department of Defense resulted in a formal reprimand by the Minister of Religion.

My unrelenting struggle to reform the State Church from within finally became more than I could endure, and in 1893 I resigned from the ministry and became administrator of an Adult Education Facility. This provided me with a more advantageous place from which to express my liberal religious views. I wrote many articles which were regularly published in the leading Copenhagen newspaper.

It was also during this period of my life that I became acquainted with the lectures and publications of Kristofer Jansen, who (as you know) had established a Unitarian Church in Norway at this same time.

In 1898 my wife and I moved to Copenhagen and began the publication of *Lys over Landet*, in English that is *Light over the Land*. It was a journal of liberal religious thought.

The influential editor, Theo Berg heard one of my lectures and almost immediately became my most ardent supporter. I was having considerable difficulty with my hearing at that time. This did not hinder my public speaking, but did make it difficult for me to negotiate lecture tours. Berg took over this responsibility and made it possible for me to take my message to much greater numbers of people.

In 1900 Theo and his good friend Mary Westenholtz organized the Free Church Society (Unitarian) in Copenhagen and named me as its minister.

The next year I published a book, *Troen og det utrolige* or *Belief and the Unbelievable*. It was essentially a treatise about truth and honesty. I pointed out that agnosticism, an acceptance of the fact that we do not know, was the only honest response to questions about either the origins of life or the conclusion of life. We simply know nothing about the first or the last link in the chain of life. We may speculate. We may theorize. We may accept some things on faith. But we do not know.

Naturally, the official leaders of the State Church could not accept this challenge to their dogmatic assertions or claims to be the respository of Religious Truth. On the other hand there were many members of the clergy who were comfortable with our challenge to orthodoxy. It was not infrequent that these friends were guest speakers at our services.

There were enough of them to lead Mary Westenholz and I to believe that one of our missions was to assist the State Church in becoming open and tolerant enough to encompass Unitarian views. As Mary has recently told you, that was a dream which came to naught.

We were accused of being destructive. "You can only tear down, not build up," was the judgment. To this I responded: "Dear fellow citizens, this is indeed a hard accusation, and I admit it would be crushing, were it true in the sense that we believe in nothing, and just wish to level the old faith to the ground. But we tear down only that original truth and beauty can be revealed."

When a malignancy is formed on our body, then the surgeon must remove it. But nothing need to be placed in its stead save the reestablished health, which is itself older than the malignancy.

When different parasitic plants threaten to kill a tree, they must be removed so the sun and air can do their healing. Nothing needs to be put in their place except the released life-giving energy which now flows through its stem and branches.

When an old beautiful cathedral is scarred by later unfitting extensions or whitewashings, then one would tear down and erase these abominations so the temple can emerge in its original pure style. Nothing is needed other than its intrinsic beauty.

Who tore down more than Jesus? Was he not accused of destroying the Law and the Prophets? It was true. He removed many of the human inventions which had accumulated over the years and obscured the purity of ethical monotheism. He broke down walls of separation which allowed the God of Israel to be known to the nations.

As you can see, I considered myself to be a Christian. I know that Unitarianism has evolved into a much more inclusive faith-community in your day, but in my lifetime my views differed little from those of my contemporaries in the Unitarian churches of Great Britain and America.

I remained with the congregation in Copenhagen for eighteen years. Finally, almost completely deaf and crippled by rheumatism, I retired and turned leadership of our congregation over to my protégé Thorvald Kierkegaard. He has his own story to tell.

God Morgen. Mit navn er

ANTON M. JENSEN

You have invited me here today to affirm my Credo, my basic beliefs. That can be most easily expressed, I think, by repeating what I once told the Bishops of the Lutheran (State) Church in Denmark.

"We can no longer cling to Luther. We need a giant who has the strength to kick all the dogmas back into the mouldy study-corner from where they came, and we need a cleaning woman who can scrub all the dirt off the windows, so the rest of us can see God again."

That is clear and concise enough, is it not?

But I suppose I should tell you a bit more about how I reached that critical moment in my life, and what I did in the years which followed.

My father was a Lutheran pastor of decidedly fundamentalist leanings. Growing up in the parsonage, and reared by devout and loving parents, my own decision to study for the ministry was a surprise to no one.

Still, on the completion of my seminary studies and ordination, I was determined to be my own person and not merely a carbon-copy of my father. In a variety of ways I declared my independence and informed my bishop that I did not wish to be type-cast in one way or the other. The bishop responded by deliberately assigning me to a parish in a small, remote fishing village noted for its orthodoxy.

Very shortly after my arrival to assume my pastoral duties I received a visit from a delegation of older members, whose mission was to explain to me exactly how they intended me to perform. Obviously they had been notified by the ecclesiastical authorities that I was something of a non-conformist and needed to be brought under control.

In as friendly a way as possible, I responded by telling them that I could not, and would not, teach or preach anything which my personal conscience did not find right. My answer did not meet with their approval.

Deciding that I probably would not be able to reach the older members, I turned my attention to the young. I converted the upstairs of the parsonage into a library, which in a short time became a favorite meeting place for our younger members. Open discussions, on subjects of interest to them, were regular events. Rather than being welcomed, these activities were condemned as "secular" and not the business of a pastor.

What really got me in trouble, however, was the preaching of my ideas about a loving God and the improbability of the reality of Hell. It seemed to me, and I said so openly, that the concepts of a loving Father and of eternal punishment were contradictory ideas. I had not at this time in my life ever heard of the Universalist Church, but we certainly held similar beliefs.

Protests to the District Bishop brought a letter of reprimand. I was instructed to adhere closely to the State Church's official interpretation of Scripture. He also instructed me to read the letter of reprimand to my congregation on the following Sunday. I refused to do so. In my letter of reply I explained that I felt it inappropriate to read a statement in which the Bishop approved of people suffering eternal torture in Hell.

An almost continuous flow of complaints from orthodox members of the congregation made their way to the District Bishop, followed by additional letters of reprimand. I continued to ignore or defy them all.

Finally, in November 1900, after I had publicly called the official views of the Church on the matter of Hell to be "abominable," the matter of my heresy was referred to the Guiding Church Council, which consisted of all the Bishops. They decreed that I was to be notified that it was entirely unacceptable for a minister to contradict the official teaching of the Church.

I would probably have been "dismissed" at that time except that I had found an earlier declaration by the same Council which said that "the problem of eternal damnation remains an open question within the teaching of the evangelical church. It is undoubtable that an eternal Hell exists, but it is permissible to hope it does not."

I found it difficult to debate with Bishops whose arguments were founded on such highly intellectual logic.

In a lecture three weeks later, I issued the statement which I began this morning. Remember? The need for a giant to kick out the dogmas and a cleaning woman to scour the windows so we could see God. The official papers of my dismissal from the ministry followed shortly.

Two years earlier Kristofer Janson, founder of the Unitarian Church in Norway, had established a congregation in Aarhus, Denmark which he often visited on holiday. He was only able to give part-time leadership since his major responsibility was in Christiania.

I was invited to assume the pastoral duties of this congregation. It was an offer I accepted with great joy. For the next five years I enjoyed the unspeakable privilege of a free pulpit, where I could speak from my conscience without fear of ecclesiastical rebuke.

After a half-decade, however, I grew restless. The congregation was quite loving and accepting, but also quite small. I yearned for a larger audience for the message I felt constrained to declare.

I chose, therefore, to resign that ministry and become a lecturer for Adult Education School and Programs. That brought me into contact with a much wider range of the population which I saw in need of a message of spiritual liberation.

I hope I was able to dislodge some antiquated dogmas of the mind and wash some windows of the soul.

God Morgen. Jeg er

THORVALD KIERKEGAARD

Right at the beginning let me assure that I am not related to the renowned existentialist Soren Kierkegaard. Our shared surname is relatively common in Denmark.

Besides, he encouraged those seeking religious truth to make a "great leap of faith." On the other hand, as the long-time minister of Copenhagen's Unitarian Church, I urged people to exercise reason in the spiritual quest.

I did not start out as a free-thinker. That came later.

My father was a highly respected educator, the Director of a School for Adult Education. As a child in the latter years of the 19th century I remember him reading the poetry of Uffe Birkedal to me and my siblings.

On one occasion Birkedal was invited to speak at an alumni event at father's school. It was a thrilling experience. From that day on I was a great admirer of this man whom I would ultimately follow in leadership of the Copenhagen congregation, even though I knew nothing of his liberal religious views at that time.

My own youthful religious yearnings prompted me to pursue a theological education after my graduation from high school. Fortunately, long before I would have been ready for ordination I realized that the dogmatic interpretation of the Scriptures held by the State Church would make it impossible for me to pledge the oath required of those entering the clergy. I could not have done so with integrity.

It was not until 1910, when I was thirty-one years old, that I became acquainted with Unitarianism. My wife and I had moved to Aarhus, Denmark's second largest city, where a Free Society had been convened a decade earlier. You will recall Kristofer Janson telling of establishing a congregation there.

P. P. Hoegsted was the minister at the time, and I very quickly discovered that his interpretation of religion was almost exactly what I had earlier discerned on my own. Until that moment I did not know it had a name or that there were others who shared similar views. My years of soul-searching seemed to have led me to a friendly shore.

Two years later I had the good fortune to meet Uffe Birkedal at the General Assembly of the Unitarian Congregation of Aarhus.

On that occasion the members of the Aarhus congregation hosted a picnic for our guests from Copenhagen. Each family was asked to bring a basket lunch and to invite one of our visitors to join them for the meal. My wife and I were not officially members yet, so we waited while others made their choices. One middle-aged woman appeared to be left and we invited her to share with us. It turned out to be Mary Westenholz, a founder of the Free Society movement and one of the most famous women in Denmark. Neither my wife nor I had ever met her, but were both familiar with her writings.

Wonderful things happen in the most unusual ways. Before the picnic was over Miss Westenholz had convinced me to give up my profession as a lecturer and organize and direct a Unitarian Adult School. Adult Schools are something of a Danish phenomenon. Classes are established to meet specific needs. They may last one week or several months. They are strictly for learning. There are no examinations, no grades, no degrees. They are simply designed for the enrichment of our people.

Before long P. P., Uffe, and Mary all joined forces to encourage me to return to seminary and get a theological education so that I might organize a third Unitarian congregation. It took me six long years, but in 1918 I received my degree. The completion of my studies coincided with a serious decline in the health of Uffe Birkedal. He had been deaf for some time, but now his body was ravaged by rheumatism which made it impossible for him to continue his ministerial duties.

I was asked to succeed him and even though I felt it quite presumptuous of me to even consider attempting to follow such a scholar and saint, I agreed and began a ministry which would continue for forty-seven years.

When I took over leadership the congregation did not have its own permanent meeting place and made frequent moves from one rented facility to another. One of my priorities was the establishment of a Building Fund which resulted in the 1927 construction of the magnificent Unitarernes Hus . . . The House of the Unitarians.

Many generous contributions, not the least of which came from Nina Grieg, made this possible.

One of the proudest moments of my life was when we hosted the 1934 convention of the International Association for Religious Freedom with meetings both in Unitarernes Hus and the Danish Parliament Building.

My preaching during those years was a liberal Christian Unitarianism, not unlike that expressed by Janson, Emerson and Parker. Our congregation was largely in accord with this approach. But I think I went farther than many others of that era in reaching out to people of other faiths. I had particularly good relations with members of the Jewish community of Denmark.

Like my friend and mentor Kristofer Janson and his wife, I was open to the exploration of Spiritualism which was quite popular at that time. With the congregation's approval I made the down-stairs meeting room in our building available to the Spiritualistic Church.

In my later years I seriously studied the eastern religions and was deeply influenced by them. Particularly, I explored the concept of reincarnation, which seemed to me to be as reasonable an assumption as any traditional Christian view of an afterlife.

So, I was intimately associated with the Unitarian movement in Denmark through the major portion of the 20th century. Following my nearly 50 years of service, the congregation had a series of ministers who turned out to be merely liberal Lutherans not genuine Unitarians. The lay members then chose to assume leadership and they have continued as a vibrant fellowship until this day.

Good Morning. I am

GEORGE DE BENNEVILLE

I was born in England of French parentage, and introduced the gospel of Universalism to America.

My father was a French nobleman who was banished to England because of assistance which he had given the Huguenots. In London, where I was born, he was employed in the Court of King William.

My mother died giving me birth as her ninth child in five years of marriage, having delivered four sets of twins before me. Queen Anne took me under her care and raised me as her own.

At the age of twelve it was determined that I should learn navigation and was sent to sea in a fleet bound for the Barbary Coast. While docked at the port of Algiers I experienced one of the major turning points in my life. Some Moors came aboard and one slipped and injured his leg quite severely. The others gathered about, kissed his wounds, wept bitter tears, and called upon the God of the Sun to bring healing to their fallen brother.

My first reaction was one of condescension and anger. Their pagan prayers filled me with disgust. Then, I looked again as they ministered to the injured one, and a great sense of shame filled my soul. My eyes filled with tears and I cried out: "Are these heathens? No. I confess before God they are Christians and I myself am the heathen." God had chosen to use the compassion of black persons, whom I believed to be inferior, to display for me the true meaning of divine love.

For many months afterward I was overcome with deep melancholy, feeling there was no hope for my salvation. But, at last, in a heavenly vision I came to know that God in His holy love for all creatures will save all the human species.

I was convinced that it was my duty to proclaim this universal love. At age 17 I forsook my life of luxury in the English court and sailed to France where I began preaching wherever people gathered: in the market place, in forests, in private homes. Time and again I was arrested and jailed for heresy.

As more and more persons were drawn to the doctrines I was declaring, the authorities grew more threatened. Along with another young friend, George M. Durant, I was arrested. We were tried, convicted of heresy, and sentenced to death. His penalty was the gallows. Because I was of noble birth I was to be beheaded. The guillotine was not used for those born commoners.

I watched as my friend sang the 126th Psalm as he climbed the ladder to his gallows. Then, even after my head had been placed on the block, a courier arrived from King Louis XV, with a reprieve. I was remanded to prison where I remained for several months before being released on the insistence of the Queen.

Still fearing for my life if I remained in France, I went to Germany where I spent the next 18 years. While continuing to preach at every opportunity, I also engaged in the study of medicine and qualified to become a physician.

There were a great variety of small religious sects in both Germany and Holland with whom I found areas of common agreement. Groups such as the Anabaptists, Seekers of Light, Philadelphians, Spiritualists, and others who gave me a hospitable hearing.

After two centuries, or so, of persecution many from these and similar groups had migrated to the New World. In 1741, my 38th year, I decided to join them, and sailed for Pennsylvania.

I took up residence in Germantown and was befriended by a Quaker printer named Christopher Sower. Together we translated and published in English a book by Paul Siegman entitled *The Everlasting Gospel*. First published in Germany in 1700, this book was an exposition of Universalist ideas. Our English translation became a major instrument in the planting and growth of Universalism on the North American continent.

Next I moved to the Oley Valley, some forty miles northwest of Philadelphia. At the same time I was married to Esther, the daughter of a Huguenot family from Germany. When we were married my bride was 25 and I sixteen years her senior.

I taught school, preached, and practiced medicine. I supported my wife and our five children with small fees I charged for my medical practice. I refused to accept any money for teaching or preaching.

Twice each year from then until I was an old man, I traveled far and wide to spread the gospel of Universalism. My journeys took me to western Pennsylvania, Maryland and Virginia. Converts on their western migration took the message throughout the frontier.

Frequent friendly contacts with American Indians gave me additional opportunity to practice what I believed about God's love for all his creation. Others may have believed, as was often said, that, "the only good Indian is a dead Indian," but to me they were beloved members of the human family.

I studied their language and constructed a dictionary of Indian words with both English and German translations, in an effort to encourage communication between the different peoples who inhabited the region.

I cherished the relationships I established with their Medicine Men, sharing with them my medical knowledge, and learning from them of the healing qualities of many herbs and plants of which I had been ignorant.

After more than a decade in the Oley Valley, we moved to Philadelphia where our children could have access to a better education. There I developed a close friendship with both Benjamin Franklin and Dr. Benjamin Rush.

During the Revolutionary War my two sons served in the Continental Army. Even though I was 75 years of age at the time of the Battle of Germantown, I ministered to the wounded and dying of both the American and British armies. I had believed too deeply for too long to deny at that point in my life the worth of every human life.

I never stopped preaching until my death at age 79 in 1782. I never built a church. I never organized a denomination. But Universalism was established in America through my efforts. Blessed be the name of the Lord forever.

Good Morning. I am

JOHN MURRAY

I came into this world in the year 1741 in Hampshire, England, the eldest son of an Anglican father and a Presbyterian mother. Though they were of separate denominations, both were rigid Calvinists. My childhood was not a happy one. Indeed, it was not intended to be. Calvinists believed that all people, even children, should spend their days in fearful contemplation of the eternal punishment that awaited all but the few "elect" of God.

Life improved after the family migrated to Cork, Ireland when I was a lad of ten. There my father came under the influence of the Methodists and John Wesley himself was a frequent visitor in our home. Mr. Wesley took a great interest in me and often said that his only fear was that I had imbibed too deeply of my father's damnable Calvinistic principles.

In time I returned to London, found employment in a mill, and became active in the Tabernacle where the Methodist evangelist George Whitefield preached to great crowds. It was there I met, wooed, won and married Eliza Neal. The courtship was not without its obstacles, however. Eliza lived with her grandfather who hated Methodists and would permit none to enter his house. Eliza and I met before dawn each day to attend 5 a.m. services at the Tabernacle, permitting her to be back home in time to prepare her grandfather's breakfast before he had risen for the day.

There was another preacher in London at that time who was also attracting great public interest. He was James Relly who proclaimed a doctrine of Universal Salvation. When a young woman from our Tabernacle seemed to have accepted this Relly heresy, I was assigned the task of meeting with her and convincing her of the error of her ways. But just the opposite occurred. Her arguments were so convincing, and my inability to respond so embarrassing that I claimed a prior appointment and removed myself from her presence.

My wife and I determined that we should go hear this man for ourselves and so on a Sunday when Whitefield was away from London, we did so. It was reported back to the leadership of the Tabernacle that we had attended a service of the blasphemous Relly and we were dismissed from their fellowship.

We then associated ourselves with the followers of Reverend Relly—then called Rellites—and I frequently preached when he was speaking elsewhere.

Life then took a bitter turn. Our first child became ill and died before his first birthday and my beloved wife never recovered from the melancholy of her loss. After a lengthy period of illness she also died, leaving me with a broken heart and huge debts incurred while trying to care for her. Life lost all purpose for me. Even when arrested and thrown into debtor's prison, I was indifferent to my condition.

Upon my eventual release I was urged by James Relly to forget my selfish sorrow and serve others by preaching the new doctrine of hope. My response was that I only wished to pass through life unheard, unseen, unknown to all, as though I had never been.

In order to do so I decided to remove myself to America, which was in those days the equivalent of going out of the world. In July 1770, I set sail on a brig heading for New York. No one other than the beneficent God himself could predict what would unfold before me in that new land.

As we neared the American coast a storm drove us off course and we were grounded on a sandbar in a little bay called Cranberry Inlet near what is now Good Luck, New Jersey. I took a small boat and went ashore seeking provisions for the crew.

There I came upon a man named Thomas Potter who offered me a great quantity of fish without charge. He said that he had not paid for the fish when he took them from the sea and would accept no payment for giving them to others.

He then took me into a deep grove of trees on his property, where to my amazement I beheld a beautiful and spacious Meeting House. He told me that years earlier he had by himself reached the conclusion that a loving God would not condemn anyone to eternal damnation, and had built the Meeting House as a place where this gospel could be proclaimed. Like Noah who had built an Ark when there was no hint of rain, he had suffered from years of ridicule by his neighbors. But he had never lost faith that one day God would send a messenger to preach in that place. Furthermore, he told me that he perceived me to be that one. I responded that while I had, indeed, preached at one time in my life, I was determined to do it no more.

But he persisted, pleading with me to stay until the following Sunday and fill the pulpit of his chapel. When I responded that I intended to sail as soon as the wind changed and lifted our boat from the sandbar, he said that the wind would never change until I had agreed to preach.

As he had predicted, the wind did not change. I did preach the message of Universal Love and Salvation to an amazed congregation of neighbors who crowded the Meeting House to overflowing. And I never stopped preaching for the next forty-five years.

For a short time I lived with Thomas Potter and ministered to the congregation he had gathered. Then I began missionary journeys which took me into New England. In Gloucester, Massachusetts I found a small group of people who were adherents of Relly's theology and settled with them. There I met and married Judith Sargent, whose intellectual achievements surpassed my own. I could tell you so much about her, but it is better that I permit her to speak for herself at another time.

There were scattered groups of Universalists in Pennsylvania, New Jersey, New York and elsewhere, but their efforts were not coordinated in any way. I was instrumental in convening a conference at Oxford, Massachusetts in 1775, which resulted in the formation of the Universalist denomination in America.

After two decades in Gloucester, I moved on to the First Universalist Church in Boston where I spent the rest of my life. On an earlier visit to that city attempts had been made to forbid me to speak. Stones were thrown through the window of the auditorium. When one rather large one barely missed my head, I held it up and announced to the congregation, "This argument is weighty, but not convincing. Not all the stones in Boston, except they stop my breath, shall shut my mouth." And, they never did.

> Go out into the highways and by-ways
> Give people something of your new vision.
> You may possess a small light, but uncover it.
> Let it shine.
> Use it in order to bring more light and understanding
> to the hearts and minds of men and women.
> Give them not hell, but hope and courage.
> Preach the kindness and everlasting love of God.

Good Morning. I am

JUDITH SARGENT MURRAY

My second husband, whom I married after the death of my first, was John Murray who brought Universalism to America from England.

I was born in 1751, in Gloucester, Massachusetts, into a family of considerable wealth.   My father, Winthrop Sargent, was a shipowner and merchant. As well, he was a man of liberal ideas who was determined that his daughter should be educated along with his son.   So, in my early years I received a classical education. Later, however, tutors were brought in to prepare my brother for matriculation at Harvard, and my training was redirected to the domestic arts. Nevertheless, my brother shared with me the fruits of his special tutoring, and even continued to do so on his school breaks during his university years.

While I always regretted not having been permitted to enjoy the blessings of attending college, I, nonetheless, made sure that my intellect was never made subservient to the demands of the kitchen and the sewing room. I may not have had a tutor (other than my brother), but I did have access to the extensive library in my father's house.

From an early age I was a voluminous writer. In my teens I wrote poetry. In my early twenties I was publishing essays on politics, religion, the role of women in society. I wrote a regular column for the *Massachusetts Magazine* entitled *The Gleaner*. In 1795 I wrote the play *The Medium, or A Happy Tea Party*, which was produced at the Federal State Theatre in Boston. It was the first play by an American author ever produced there.

Letter writing was one of the joys of my life. It was not uncommon for men of stature such as Washington, Adams, Jefferson, and the like to keep copies of all their correspondence, but women did not do so. But I did! From a very early age, I laboriously copied and saved every letter I wrote. During my lifetime I preserved in Letter Books over 2,500 copies of my extensive correspondence.

My writings covered many subjects, but none was so important as those dealing with the role of women in society. My most famous work, possibly, is an essay entitled *On the Equality of the Sexes*. My thesis was that women possessed an intellect which could not be satisfied by the needle and the kitchen. Any perceived intellectual differences between women and men were the result of differences in expectation and training. If equal education was available the difference would disappear.

Having just fought and won a war of Independence from England, the new nation was struggling to define the nature and limits of the liberty, which had been achieved. I argued as forcefully as I could against the thought that liberty was the sole possession of those who owned property and thus could prove a competency for maintaining freedom. This point of view, held by many, would have condemned slaves and women to everlasting servitude. My proposal for universal liberation, by the way, antedated Margaret Fuller's espousal of women's rights by more than a generation.

I should tell you, I suppose, that *On The Equality of Women* was written from a secular point of view. The orthodox religionists attacked me with ferocity for not dealing sufficiently, from their vantage point, with the Biblical view that sin entered the world because of Eve and that woman's inferiority and subservience to men was the inevitable result. I added an appendix to the second edition which said, in part: "Yes, ye Lordly, ye haughty sex, our souls are by nature equal to yours; the same breath of God animates, enlivens, and invigorates us: and we have not fallen lower than yourselves . . . ."

But I was to share with you more about my life, was I not?

At eighteen I married a sea captain named John Stevens. After 15 years I was widowed. My intention was to remain single and dedicate my life to the Universalist religion, which had been adopted by both my father and myself. A small group of seekers after this new doctrine of Everlasting Love and universal salvation met at my father's house for several years, and then he built what was, most likely, the first Universalist Meeting House in America.

During this time I had met the Reverend John Murray, and we had corresponded on several occasions. He had lost his wife some two decades earlier, and like myself, had vowed never to remarry. But marry we did, in 1788 and shared more than a quarter of a century together.

John not only approved of my writings and involvement in civic as well as religious affairs, but strongly encouraged me to press forward. Since we shared similar ideas on so many issues, both secular and sacred, we made a formidable team. Whether it was the struggle to achieve and preserve the separation of Church and State, the passion for the education of women, or the declaration of the Universalist gospel, we were as one.

We traveled extensively throughout the eastern states establishing and nourishing Universalist congregations, as well as ministering to the church in Gloucester, and later the First Universalist Church of Boston.

There were those who felt I was too outspoken in my solidarity with John. Universalists were free-thinkers, and there were inevitable differences of opinion on many subjects. My husband had sharp differences with Hosea Ballou, a much younger man who had emerged as the new generation leader of the liberal movement. Ballou was a "determinist." He believed that God had ordained all persons to be saved, and thus did away with free will. John thought otherwise. There is no need to re-hash this old argument today. But it mattered much back then.

The difference did not keep my husband from inviting Ballou to fill his pulpit during one ten week period when he was away visiting other churches. On the final Sunday that Rev. Ballou preached I felt it necessary to send a note up to the Choirmaster, requesting that he read it at the conclusion of the service. He followed my instructions, and before Ballou could announce the closing hymn, the Choirmaster read: "The congregation should know that the doctrine preached the past ten Sundays is not the doctrine usually preached in this house."

My actions were the occasion of considerable scandal and disapproval by many, but I always believed it was important to say what one intended regardless of the consequences.

After John's death in 1815, I left Boston and spent my remaining five years with my daughter and her husband on their estate in Natchez, Mississippi.

Good Morning. I am

DAVID PIETER FAURE

I was the founder of the Free Protestant Church of Cape Town, South Africa in 1867, which was a Unitarian congregation.

There was little in my early life that would have indicated the development. My parents were Afrikanners of Huguenot ancestry. My father, Abraham, was the Magistrate in Stilenbosch, and my mother, Dorothea was the daughter of a wine farmer at Banhoek.

The family moved to Cape Town in 1846, when I was only three years old. It was there I spent my entire life, except for a few years of study at the University of Leiden in the Netherlands.

My religious upbringing was unexceptional. At home I received the ordinary orthodox education. We were members of the Dutch Reformed Church, regularly attending it twice every Sunday. We all believed the accepted and popular doctrines; doubts were foreign to us, the Bible and the Creeds were simply accepted as infallible, because we had been taught to regard them as such. We had never heard of anyone, within the Dutch Reformed Church, who denied it.

Not until I enrolled to study for the ministry at Leiden, that is. I should tell you that Leiden was infamous among the Dutch Reformed of South Africa because of its liberal views. Our ministers were trained at the more orthodox seminaries at Ultrecht or Edinburgh. I was drawn to Leiden by what I have described as "a Mysterious Power." Plus, I am sure, the fact that it was where my father had studied law.

I will confess, even now, that I was initially horrified to hear from my fellow students that the Bible was not infallible; that it was of human origin; and that it should be read and judged the same as any other book. My two favorite professors were, actually, advanced Unitarians. One of them encouraged my study of the writings of the American Unitarian preacher Theodore Parker.

By the time I had qualified to be ordained a minister of the Dutch Reformed Church, I knew that my newly discovered Unitarian beliefs would never be accepted back home in Cape Town. Nevertheless, I accepted an invitation to preach a "trial sermon" at the Mother Church soon after my return.

Knowing that my reputation for modernist views had preceded me, I made every effort to be inoffensive. But I did not succeed. Every word I spoke was construed to be heresy. When the sermon ended, and I waited in the vestry, the visiting clergy and church wardens refused to even enter the same room with me to pick up their hats and coats.

If I wanted to preach, and indeed I did, it would be necessary for me to establish my own free pulpit. In August 1867 I rented the Mutual Assurance Society Hall for a Sunday morning service. No one asked me to do this, or had even suggested it to me. I did it completely on my own, hiring the hall at my own expense. I was confident that the collection at the door would defray the costs, and this expectation was fully justified.

My message was three fold: The Fatherhood of God, the Brotherhood of all men, and the striving after perfection. Please, dear women, forgive my sexist language. I would do better, I assure you, if I were preaching in your era.

For me the Fatherhood of God meant that God was loving, not judgmental or cruel. If God really is a Father, I said, the doctrine of eternal punishment is a monstrous lie, the doctrine of atonement another, and the doctrine of predestination yet another.

I pointed out that preachers claiming to speak for Christianity taught that those who disagreed with them were heretics and should be shunned. I said that if we taught what Jesus did we would embrace all as brothers whether they were Jews, Catholics, Protestants or Mohammedans.

As for striving for perfection, I said it was as clear as the noonday sun that if the human race were totally depraved and incapable of doing anything good, the idea of trying to be good would never enter our minds. But we do strive to do better and be better, which contradicts the doctrine of depravity.

I am not going to waste your time by reciting details of the opposition we faced from the orthodox church. Suffice it to say that we were relentlessly attacked both from the pulpit and in the public press. Most predicted that our fledgling movement would last only a few months and then disappear as the novelty diminished, and the sinister nature of our teachings became more clearly understood by the populace.

Not content to wait and see if their predictions would come true, active campaigns of opposition were waged against us. Some leaders of the Dutch Reformed Church even tried to get the Attorney General to arrest and prosecute me for heresy.

They said we would attract only the frivolous, but the truth is that we attracted a number of prominent and educated families as well as those of the working class. We never grew large in numbers, but we were great in influence, even from the beginning.

The congregation was never able to provide complete financial support for me and my family, so I periodically worked in other jobs. I served as an interpreter for the courts and for the Parliament, a journalist for a number of publications. As an editor of *Het Volksblad* I had a platform from which to speak for liberal politics and social justice.

I told you earlier that I had been introduced in my seminary days to the ideas of Theodore Parker, but I want to assure that the founding of the Free Protestant Church was accomplished independently of any Unitarian association anywhere else in the world. It was an indigenous religious group founded by South Africans of European descent.

Good Morning. I am

ROBERT STEYN

I served as minister of the Cape Town, South African Unitarian congregation from 1982 to 1997. You will recognize those dates as years of great change in my country. I count it a privilege to have had the opportunity to be a part of the awe-inspiring transformation.

Although I was born, in 1927, into an Afrikaan-speaking Dutch Reformed household my mind and heart evolved at an early age to move beyond that somewhat limited world. I became what some have called a "de-tribalized Afrikaaner." Those who say it mean it as a compliment, but I want to add that there are many parts of my heritage in which I take great pride.

More than half of my working life was spent as a journalist. I wrote for *The Argus*, which was Cape Town's English language newspaper. Our publication was well known for its political liberalism and its opposition to Apartheid. These positions were praised by a few and censured by most.

My strongly held views on these matters often brought me into contact with members and leaders of the Unitarian Church. I found in that fellowship an oasis of acceptance and support. My mind was stimulated by the appeal to reason. My soul was refreshed in the companionship of others who shared my sense of right and wrong. Shortly after my thirtieth birthday I officially became a Unitarian.

About five years later, in 1967, our minister Victor Carpenter resigned and returned to America. He was the person who had first introduced me to liberal religion and had often encouraged me to consider making a career change and becoming a minister. It was an idea that held considerable interest for me. Rev.

Carpenter believed that it was important that the Cape Town congregation have "one of its own" as a minister, rather than another import from America. So, at his urging, I applied for the position to succeed him. Many of our members were supportive of my candidacy, but our Church Constitution specified the necessity of theological educational credentials, which I lacked.

Another minister was called and I remained with the newspaper. But I not only remained in the church, I probably expanded my involvement after that. I taught in the Sunday school and served on a number of important committees. One of my activities was that of Pulpit Manager. Through it all I never gave up my dream of one day entering seminary and qualifying for the ministry.

In addition to keeping busy with local church activities, I also was called upon quite frequently to respond to articles in Unitarian Universalist publications in the United States and the United Kingdom about political matters in South Africa. I also, represented our church on the Citizen's Committee on Conscientious Objectors.

When Rev. Leon Fay, who had been our minister for nearly a decade, left to return to America in 1979, I was designated as lay preacher. The next year I attended Manchester College in Oxford, England and received a diploma in theological studies qualifying me to be ordained and installed as minister of the Cape Town congregation.

In my years of ministry I attempted to give my primary attention to being a pastor to the members of our congregation. Their needs came first. That does not mean, however, that I was not active in the affairs of the larger community beyond our own circle.

I took a leading role in the activities of the Cape Town Interfaith Forum and always maintained close fellowship with other organizations dedicated to justice and tolerance.

In the Apartheid era we lived under the restrictions of what was called the Group Areas Act. That statute required that separate segments of the population lived in specified areas. The purpose was to keep Black South Africans in segregated Townships. It was even illegal for residents of these areas to venture outside those designated boundaries at night, except with special permission.

When Apartheid was rejected and democracy established, the Group Areas Act was annulled. This brought great numbers of impoverished blacks into the inner city. Our church was located in the downtown section of Cape Town. I responded, as best I could, by establishing a ministry for the street people who gathered near our building on Hout Street. Food was distributed every evening.

When one of our church members was elected Mayor of Cape Town he appointed me city chaplain. One of the functions of that office was the planning and conducting of a public worship service on the annual Mayoral Sunday. Up to this time the service had been exclusively Christian, primarily Dutch Reformed.

I was determined to make it inclusive and arranged for the active participation of Jews, Muslims, and Buddhists as well as Christians. While some of the more conservative Christians complained, those who had been included for the first time were deeply appreciative of a service which did not offend their religious convictions.

Another expression of our inclusive spirit was the fact that both the Sufi's and the Christian Scientists held their first meetings in our building.

Our Unitarian approach reflected the spirit of our newly emerging nation. In all things we sought to expand democracy with hope and reconciliation.

To attempt to summarize my Credo is difficult. It probably contains three fundamental ideas:

First, to have compassion for the "underdog."

Second, to practice what I call "non-judgmentalism" and acceptance of all people.

Third, to work in a society with a sick and twisted political ideology while holding up a vision of that which is good and decent in humankind.

Those are the principles to which I was committed and to which the Unitarians of South Africa are committed.

By the way, that Mayor of Cape Town who appointed me chaplain has now succeeded me as minister of the church.

When you get the chance, come to South Africa and see for yourself what we have accomplished.

Ohayoh Gozaimasu.

AKASHI SHIGETAROH desu

I was a minister of the Liberal Christian Church of Japan for seven decades, but because I refused to accept a salary from the church it was necessary to engage in many other activities. These included the writing of many books, the first Japanese translation of Greek and Roman mythology, lectures, teaching in both public and missionary schools, innumerable lectures and speeches, and many others.

My life span, from 1872 to 1965, covered three major periods of Japanese history: Meiji, Taisho, and Showa. I lived through the Sino-Japanese War of 1894-95, the Russo-Japanese War of 1904-05, World Wars I and II, and experienced the Great Kanto Earthquake of 1923.

My tribulations were many. In one short period I lost my wife and all but one of my ten children. My only consolation was the similar experience of the Biblical character, Job. Like him, I declared, "Yea, though He slay me, yet will I trust Him."

But let me go back to the beginning. I was born in the prefecture of Fukuoka, the first son of Jinkichi and Sai Akashi. For many generations the Akashi men had been Sword Masters, the highest rank of samurai.

My father wanted me to become a doctor, but I was determined to enter politics. When I was 15, father became convinced that I was serious about this and permitted me to move to our capitol city and enroll in Tokyo English School. From there I moved up to Tokyo College where I began my studies in Political Science, which was taught in the English language. My motivation for choosing politics as a career was because I felt it would be the instrument through which I could do something about the terrible poverty of our people. From earliest childhood I had been deeply troubled by the suffering I saw all around me.

Up to this time I had been indifferent to religion. Our family had only engaged in religious activities of a cultural and patriotic kind. Then I was befriended by a young Christian man, named Saitoh, who invited me to attend his church with him. The more I learned about Christianity the more I became convinced that it, too, could help me in finding a remedy for poverty and pain. At age 18, I was baptized a Christian, withdrew from Tokyo College and enrolled in the Evangelical Protestant divinity school. My deeply disappointed father withdrew all financial support.

I became acquainted with the leaders of a seminary run by the Universalist Church, and took some classes, and even did some teaching there. In 1893, I graduated from seminary with a degree in systematic theology, having already published both books and Biblical translations.

After graduation I began my ministry in Nagoya, knowing that Buddhism was deeply rooted there, but determined to avoid the mistakes for which I had earlier criticized missionaries. Their most grievous errors, it seemed to me, were treating the Japanese people as savages, or merely showing pity for them, and claiming that Christianity was the only true religion. I knew that both of these things were wrong. Wrong, both morally and intellectually.

I spent eleven years there and did much, I believe, in moderating the prejudice, which many held against Christianity. It was there I found my wife, Shizuko Kiwaki, and began our family.

Then I returned to Tokyo to become minister of the Tokyo Universalist Church. Newly arrived Universalist missionaries from abroad were rather conservative and found my liberal views more than they could tolerate. I was forced to leave and to close the school I had organized for the education of women and girls. Fortunately, the Universalists became less rigid in their theology in later years and we were able to work together in many things.

After an interval of teaching, lecturing, and writing I joined with four friends in the organization of a new congregation, which was accepting of my liberal views.

This phase of my life coincided with a period of great social upheaval in Japan. The new 20th century brought the development of industry, labor unrest, and an ever greater disparity between the rich and the poor. Many of our citizens turned to Socialism as a solution, and I counted myself among them. I viewed Socialism as the secular partner of Christianity. I heard in its plea for equality, racial and economic justice, and international cooperation an echo of the teachings of Jesus.

In 1910 an attempt was made to assassinate the Emperor. Hundreds of suspected Socialists were arrested and many executed. All documents suspected of advocating Socialism were confiscated and banned. This reign of terror grew more intense during World War I. Anyone suspected was arrested by a special police force called Tokkoh. Because of my writings and speeches I was on the government's "black list" and was frequently visited by Tokkoh. Each time I thought I would be taken away, but it never happened.

The years immediately following that war were those I mentioned earlier, the time of my great personal loss. With God's grace I survived that time of testing and continued with my mission of presenting the story of a benevolent Creator and a Gospel of Love to my countrymen. Our church was destroyed in the Great Earthquake, but we were able to rebuild five years later. I was supported through this by my second wife, Chiu.

In 1928 full power was given to the Japanese military to stamp out not only Communism and Socialism, but also any expression of liberalism or pacifism. One part of the new law placed all religious bodies under the direct control of the government.

My last book which had been entitled *Liberal Christianity* was banned because of the use of the word "liberal." It was later republished with the name *Pure Christianity*.

One of our important contributions at this time was providing headquarters for the first national labor movement and assisting in founding the Social Democratic Party.

During the Second World War our congregation was nearly destroyed. Our people lost their shelters and were starved, but Chiu and I vowed to begin again as soon as it was possible.

After the war one of the American translators, assigned to the Tokyo International Military Trial, was a Unitarian. When he learned there was a liberal Christian movement in Japan he came to see me. This led to the creation of the Japanese Free Religion Union, comprised of four bodies including the Unitarians and Universalists. The unifying principle was to: "Ignite the idea of religion in human hearts, enrich their spiritual lives, and by carrying them along, strive for actualizing the ideal society."

Guten Morgen. Ich bin

RUDOLF WALBAUM

Born in 1869, the son of a clergyman, in the northern Germany town of Egestorf, my boyhood was spent walking and playing among the junipers and birch trees in the hilly heartland. My teachers opened windows for me to literature, history and philosophy. When I decided to study Lutheran theology, my parents encouraged me to follow that trail in the universities of Leipzig, Greifswald and Goettingen.

At age 27 I was serving as pastor in Hannover, but the image of Jesus and interpretation of the Bible I was presenting in my sermons were too liberal for the superintendent. He arranged a disciplinary transfer to an isolated mountain village congregation.

The established Prussian Church, with Emperor Wilhelm II as its head, was too fusty and musty for me. I sought better conditions with the Protestant minorities in the multi-ethnic Hapsburg Austria of Emperor Franz Joseph. For a while I served in the Vienna district, and later in Northern Bohemia.

A vacancy for a *Free Protestant* pastor in the Worms/Alzey Rhineland, southwest of Frankfurt, offered the opportunity to further my liberal theology. I knew from history that two decades of Napoleonic annexation on the left of the Rhine had opened minds of those people to ideas of civil rights and religious freedom. I was happy to become the fourth minister since their founding in 1876 and to benefit from their autonomy with regard to theology and finance. I assumed that position in 1909, the very year my wife, Lisa, gave birth to our only child, Rolf.

The following year I visited Berlin to attend the fifth World Conference of the *International Congress of Free Christians and Other Religious Liberals*. This was a spiritual adventure for me, as I recognized my own thinking in the words of the featured speakers.

I heard Thomas Slicer of the All Souls Church in New York City say that liberal theology should be "in thought free, in temper reverent, and in method scientific."

I heard George Boros of Transylvania declare, "I am a Unitarian. My program is: liberality in searching the truths of theology and in judging the religious opinions of others."

I was inspired by Thomas Masaryk from Prague, who later became President of the Czechoslovakian Republic, tell of the struggle for freedom and truth in Bohemia, and bring greetings from the land of Huss to the land of Luther.

I was deeply moved by the words and presence of the 35 year old Albert Schweitzer.

I left that mountaintop experience knowing that I was, and would remain, a Unitarian!

Aware of the shortage of Central European literature and research on Socinian and/or Unitarian thought during the previous three centuries, I started a quarterly in 1911: *The Free Protestant German Unitarian Leaflet.*

From Azley, during the nearly four decades of my ministry, I made several efforts to enlarge the Unitarian/Free Protestant cause in Germany. My essay, *What Is Unitarianism?*, of 1915, was well received by Clemens Taesler of the Free Religious Frankfurt community.

In the following years Taesler and I developed a cooperative working relationship and in 1927 organized the Deutscher Unitarierbund (DUB). It was not possible, however, for our separate communities to merge. An old law, dating back to the illiberal Medieval State Church, forbade the unification of smaller religions. That was because the mayor of a municipality, or the grand duke of a county, personally controlled the benefits of publicly levied church taxes for their territory.

Shortly after Hitler and the Holy See signed their concordat in July 1933, I attended a meeting of the newly founded "Association of German Minority Beliefs." This group had a very short life and was soon banned by the Nazis, as was our DUB. Surviving the war years in my congregation in Alzey was most difficult and required all the skills and strength I could muster.

When, finally, the war was over and the country was divided into four occupation zones by the Allied Forces, our congregation was blessed by being remembered and given help by both Director Herbert Hitchen of the American Unitarian Association in Boston and Magnus Ratter of the English Unitarians in London. Very soon we were acknowledged by the religious officers of the three Western military administrations. They made is possible for us to receive paper to write and publish and the freedom to travel to assemble.

These were necessary conditions because a friendly word during those months was an anchor of re-orientation for so many people. In spite of my 76 years I began to feel sprightly again, and 1946-47 became my busiest and most successful years in spreading the Unitarian message in our country. New congregations were founded and structures were adjusted to a national scale.

For pastoral care, and to help re-orient internees to their main-stream churches, many Catholic priests and Protestant pastors, visited the internment camps where the Allies were trying to re-educate the National Socialist Party members, if it seemed their involvement in Nazi activities had surpassed a certain level. I was also permitted to go in, and as a consequence, I would guess, about one third of the newly gained adherents to Unitarianism may have come from there.

A democratic future of the movement, however, requires that any remnants of totalitarian thinking, should they arise, must be over-ruled by a strong liberal majority. That could create a problem. Still, if the principle of religious freedom is well understood it should not be insurmountable.

My life ended in 1948, but my work has been validated in the succeeding years. Three associations were legally registered as Unitarian: in Frankfurt by Rev. Clemens Taseler, in Berlin by Rev. Hansgeorg Remus, a refugee from East Prussia, and my own community as Deutsche Unitarier Religionsgemeinschaft Worms/Rhein. Still later they all became members of the *International Association for Religious Freedom*, a body which hopefully will continue to strengthen the liberal-mindedness of religious minorities everywhere.

Guten Morgen. Ich bin

HANS-DIETRICH KAHL

I was born in Dresden in 1920. My father studied theology for a short time before developing an aversion to the nonsense of "school-theologians." He then studied medicine and became a doctor. Writings found after his death indicate he was a Unitarian, without ever having heard of Unitarianism.

My mother practiced a non-dogmatic, humble, and practical piety. I was sent to the children's Sunday services, but was not forced to continue when I found the stiff liturgical formulas repellent. I did, however, follow the religious teaching in the school with interest.

With Hitler's rise to power in 1933, I was first affected personally when our Boy Scout troop was disbanded. Though I had to accept it, I was outraged. Nevertheless, I became more and more caught up in the intensive government propaganda. Just the name, National Socialism, seemed to combine the two opposing parties—Nationalists and Socialists—which had disastrously ripped Germany apart. Then the German-English Naval Treaty of 1935 appeared to be a symbol of real peace politics.

I became a deputy leader in the "Junvolk," the organization for 10-14 year old boys within the Hitler Youth movement. Organized by the state, membership was required by law. Questionable policies and ideas, which I encountered, seemed to be things which my generation could correct when we reached positions of adult leadership.

It was during the war, when I was serving in the lower ranks of the Signal troops, I became aware of the criminal nature of the regime. I became anti-Nazi, but had no contact with the Resistance. After the war, I was held for a short period of internment before being released to freedom by the U.S. Army.

It was out of the question for me to return to my native region. The Soviets had taken over the area and my city had been destroyed. But I had recently married and my wife's family resided in the British Zone of Occupation. There I was able to make a new beginning. I went through a de-Nazification program with no problems. I was then permitted to take up my studies again.

For many years I had differences of opinion with the official church, which is extraordinarily influential in our country for historical reasons. Even though I was a student of the Bible and envied for my knowledge of Scripture, at age 17 I found it dishonest to continue being a member and officially left the church.

For a short period of time I was in contact with the German Faith Movement, but found it's anti-church inclinations destructive and repellant. I was seeking a religion that was positive and respectful of the opinions of others. It was then my good fortune, in 1946, to learn of the Religious Community of Free Protestants. This organization had been in existence since 1876, and it was through this contact I first learned of Unitarianism.

I met Rudolf Walbaum, whose personality impressed me deeply. He invited me to attend a supraregional meeting where I was challenged by the discussion of "Germany's Future as a Task for Religion." This gave me much broader insight than the more purely political orientation of the anti-Nazi re-education program provided by the occupation forces.

The necessity of encouraging personal responsibility, in a religious framework within a democratic society, was clearly presented as a key issue. I found myself in complete harmony with this movement which distinguished itself, not only from the mainstream churches with all their ministers and priests, but also from the authoritarian principles of National Socialism. Its unifying principle was the consistent lay-community, which, without specialized religious functionaries, should be maintained in a common voluntary effort by all its members. That was my world! That was exactly what I had been searching for!

In addition to our local efforts, I found incredible satisfaction in belonging to a community with worldwide connections. After the narrowness of the Third Reich, you cannot believe how liberating such expressions were. I made contacts with the Unitarians in America and regularly received the newsletter from the Church of the Larger Fellowship. Many personal international contacts occurred over the years. The highest point of these was a visit with the Rev. James Luther Adams. I had admired him for more that a decade, and had the privilege of meeting him shortly before his death.

I was frequently asked to go on lecture tours for our association, and thus was able to visit most of our fellowships. As an upper high school teacher of History, German and Latin, I was transferred several times to assist in other schools. This gave me the opportunity to help organize new Fellowships in Gottingen, Hameln, and Hannover.

Tensions rose in the German Unitarian community, as Rudolf Walbaum had feared they might, because some new members were clinging too closely to totalitarian ideas. These could not be reconciled with the open spirit of our free religious society. I became very active in helping resolve these conflicts and overcoming the repressive tendencies.

In 1959, on the basis of my professional publications, I was appointed a university lecturer. It has always been important to me to show that history—misused again and again as a weapon for national disagreements—could also be used as a means of international understanding. Improving relations between historians of different countries was a dream of mine. That became true when the Polish Academy of Science and Arts in Crackow chose me to become a corresponding member. For a period of time these new opportunities meant an interruption of my Unitarian activities.

At the end of the 1970's I was able to resume my leadership role in our religious community. In 1995 I retired from the Spiritual Council, but continue to write articles for periodicals and other publications.

More than five decades of conscious Unitarian living are behind me now. They have been instrumental in forming me. It is difficult to put into words how thankful I am for what I have received through this chosen path.

Guten Morgen. Ich bin

HORST PREM

I was born in 1940 in Nurnberg. I still remember the devastation of the relentless bombings and uncontrollable fires in that city in my earliest childhood. When I was three years of age, my parents decided to send me and my older sister to the home of our grand-mother in Austria, near the Mountains Rax and Schneeberg, to get us away from the inferno of Nurnberg.

In the spring of 1945, Soviet troops and tanks arrived, looking for the shortest route through the mountains to Mariazell. They took our house for use as a hospital and we were forced to find shelter in the home of a nearby farmer. After a few weeks we were able to return to our grandmother's house, although it had been greatly polluted by the Soviet troops. In October of that year, our parents took us back to Nurnberg. It was a very difficult journey because we had to pass through the Soviet zone to the U.S. zone near Salzburg.

I think I was greatly influenced by all these troubles of my first five years. First, I developed a consuming interest in airplanes. This led to my later profession and brought me to almost all of the aerospace centers of the northern hemisphere.

Second, I was stimulated to a deep interest in international law and human rights. I talked often with my parents about the reasons Hitler was able to command the support and loyalty of so many, considering all the trouble he and his policies had brought. They could only answer that in the beginning he seemed to be solving many social and economic problems and, therefore, was supported by many, including my parents themselves.

Both my father and my mother regretted their early support of the Nazis, but never tried to deny it. They were filled with disgust at the dishonesty of the claims, in the post-war years, of both the Protestant and Catholic Churches that they had opposed Hitler from the beginning. They withdrew themselves and their four children from any participation in church activities.

Later, in Nurnberg, and then in Bremen, we developed contacts with the German Unitarians. From my youth, I was inspired by the idea of self-responsibility in sharing and structuring our world. This became the dominant religious idea of my life.

It became very clear to me that the concept of human rights, as expressed by European philosophers during the Age of Enlightenment, had been severely violated by Hitler. Especially the principles of tolerance, separation of powers, and separation of Church and State had been ignored.

I made a pledge to myself that, to the best of my abilities, I would not stand aside and let any such violations occur again. This has kept me sensitive to identifying areas of common interest where we are today in the process of violating human rights.

One of those areas, it seems to me, is man-induced environmental problems. Whenever we abuse and mistreat our environment and thereby limit the possibilities for future generations, we are guilty of violating human rights.

Therefore, I felt it necessary to convince the German Unitarians to introduce an article into the German Grundgesetz that environmental protection of nature is a human right for coming generations. In 1994 the German Unitarians and allied organizations were successful in amending the German Constitution to include this provision. This took place at a time when Constitutional modifications were being made to accommodate the reunification of the East and the West areas of our country.

In this context the terrible violations of human rights in Ruanda and the former Yugoslavia influenced our Unitarian decision to support the United Nations Statute of the International Criminal Court (ICC), as well. The terrorist attacks of New York and Washington have further demonstrated the need for meaningful international law.

At the same time I supported the attempt to formulate a new European Constitution cross-referencing the International Criminal Court. It is my hope that such a Constitution can mentally bridge the gap between the philosophers of the Enlightenment and the people of today to solve social conflicts as well.

These social conflicts have been the background of the most bloody wars the world has ever seen. The excuse of solving social conflicts along with the idea of racial superiority led to the terrible human rights violations of Hitler. A cooperation strategy of the nations of Europe allowing for a variety of political and ethical/religious doctrines can be the only answer.

It is up to you to decide if my approach is an element of a Unitarian Universalist concept for the future.

Guten Morgen. Ich bin

GUNDA HARTMANN

In 1953, when I was nine years old, my little sister drowned. Even now I remember how she looked as a tiny corpse, the helpless faces of the grown-ups, and the suffering of my parents.

My memories of the funeral service are quite clear. There was a man, dressed in black, talking about God who was happy to take my sister into his flock of angels. As I was only nine I didn't really understand what he was saying, but felt that this explanation wasn't enough for me. It did not lessen my grief. It did not satisfy my desire to see my sweet little blond curly-haired sister again.

Later on I often went alone to the graveyard to play around her grave and talk with her so she could be with me in my imagination. I saw the flowers growing there, heard the birds chirping in the trees, and felt the sun and the rain. This all comforted me in a secret way, until I was chased away from my playground.

The Catholicism that surrounded me could never heal the wound in my heart. Other nameless things helped me cope: music, nature, people who loved me. These helped me to open up, to heal, to feel at home in the world again. My suffering lost some of its impact. Lightness, happiness and blossoms strengthened my temperament and a feeling of trust grew within me.

When, at the age of 15, I came into contact with the German Unitarian youth group, it was like an arrival home from a long journey. The destination had not been consciously chosen, but now I belonged. Later, I automatically became a Unitarian.

My job training as a lab technician, my early deutsche marriage and birth of three sons, created a bit of distance between myself and the organized Unitarian church. The expression of my religion took place inside me and in my everyday life. But I wanted my sons to have different religious experiences in their childhood than I had in mine. I wanted to share with them, and others, the feeling of security that one gains from the beauty of the natural world. I wanted them to be able to successfully negotiate the riddles of life and death by finding strength within themselves. I wanted these things not only for my own children, but all children as well.

I knew that if our children were to survive, we had to fight against the poisoning of our earth, water, and air. I became active in the movement to defend our environment. My faith, my Unitarian religion, gave me the motivation to do this. It was the motor that kept me going.

In 1987 I became editor of our Unitarian newsletter to provide a connecting link between our members and friends. It provided a forum in which we could share that which moved us, gave us strength, irritated or excited us. In it we could reflect not only on western cultural thought but also the culture of our daily dealings with each other. The themes chosen to write about were meant to touch on peoples' joys and concerns.

We also wanted to uncover our spiritual roots. They had been estranged, abused, and covered up by the terrible ideology of the Third Reich. There were vehement attacks against us in the 1980's, from some sources, because old Nazis were suspected of being in our organization. These attacks caused us to rethink our religious beliefs. Were there, perhaps, elite pretensions or a claim to exclusiveness? Where was the strength to take over responsibility? When must one become active in society, to work for democracy?

I felt the call to reflect upon myself and my activities time and time again. The radical Unitarian attitude, my being Unitarian was so fundamental to my being that it spurred me on. It provided me with even more drive for my activities in the Children's Protective League, for the environment, and for my family.

Then I was elected president of our religious organization. Now I could use the energy I got from my faith for my faith. The society experienced an upswing after the war when great efforts were made, old traditions discovered, and the will to rebuild was strong. Now, my generation was looking for new forms of community after having been confronted with the atrocities of the Reich and the involvement of our parent's generation.

During my presidency, we tried out old and new ways to worship, to share what we had in common, and to reinforce our sense of togetherness in a world tending toward isolated individualism. These were the reasons we founded the "Unitariauch," which was planned as a reader and reference about our collective efforts. It was published in 2000 under the title, *What Do You Really Believe?* One can read about the different strands of European thought that make up our roots, the recent developments in our post-war history, and our struggle with the basic beliefs that connect all of us Unitarians to one another.

Now I am a grandmother, who after eight years as president and fifteen years as an editor, have taken on new responsibilities. But nothing has changed my motivation. I want to say to my grandchild at the "Lebenieite"—the naming ceremony—"Life is wonderful, easy and hard, but full of mysteries. You have the power within that you need in order to love and protect and preserve life."

Good Morning. I am

GREGORIO AGLIPAY

I am grateful for the opportunity to appear before you today and tell you of a valiant, though ultimately futile, attempt to establish Unitarianism in the Philippines.

Our Pacific Archipelago of more than 7,000 islands had been dominated by the Catholic Church ever since 1551 when Magellan claimed the territory for his God and his nation, Spain.

Though overwhelmed by the superior might of the colonials, the Filipino people never wavered in their struggle for freedom and independence. We never adopted Spanish as our native language and resisted assimilation in many other ways.   Surprisingly, perhaps, the recurring independence movements over nearly five centuries commonly arose within the Church.

I was most fortunate in having the friendship of a great leader of our people. Jose Rizal y Mercado was a classmate in school, and a great influence in my life. When I was considering the study of law, it was Rizal who urged me to pursue a study of theology. I became a Catholic priest, a most advantageous position in later years. Please be patient and I will explain why.

You probably know of the Spanish-American War which essentially ended when the United States Navy took control of Manila Bay. Two years earlier my mentor Jose Rizal had been executed by the Spanish authorities for his unrelenting criticism of imperialism and demands for Philippine independence.

At the time we looked upon the Americans as our liberators. We believed they would guarantee our freedom as an independent republic. But we soon found that was not to be. We discovered that their purpose was simply to replace one colonial power with another. The American writer, Mark Twain, captured our feelings when he wrote that "many a Filipino must be saying to himself, there must be two Americas: one that sets captives free, and one that takes a captive's new freedom away from him, and picks a quarrel with him with nothing to found it on; then kills him to get his land."

The war against Spain was hardly over when we had to start another, this time against the United States. Most of you have probably never heard of this. American textbooks usually refer to it as a minor uprising. We call it the Philippine-American War.

After the U.S. Senate had voted to annex us as a territory and William Howard Taft was installed as the colonial Governor, a large group of us turned our attention to the Church. We might not have been able to achieve political freedom, but we could take control of our religious affairs.

American Protestants of many denominations ascended on us, fully believing that God had spoken to them through the sounds of Admiral Dewey's cannons in our harbor, commissioning them to claim us as their own. If you think I am being overly dramatic, you need to know that I am quoting directly from the oratory of one denominations chosen leader.

We wanted none of that. We wanted a Church that was our own, with our own leadership, and our own governance. Under the leadership of myself and my colleague Don Isabelo de los Reyes, Sr. the *Santa Iglesia Catholica Apostolica Filipina Independiente,*—the Independent Philippine Church—was born.

We adopted theological principles of our martyred leader, Jose Rizal. Even though he had never studied theology, he formulated a creed for himself, over one hundred years ago, which is strikingly similar to the seven principles of the Unitarian Universalist Church in America.

While supporting the use of reason rather than the acceptance of dogma, emphasizing deeds rather than creeds, and teaching that social responsibility and love for one's fellows was the heart of the gospel, we nonetheless held on to many worship forms from our past.

We kept from the Catholic Church all that seemed reasonable and harmless. We maintained the vestments and the magnificent ceremonies which were so beloved by our people. But we did it with a rational interpretation. What was myth to science was a myth to us.

On several occasions we sought closer fellowship with other Protestant bodies in the Philippines, but we were always rejected because they thought we were still too Catholic.

We went our independent way, and within twenty years had grown to a membership of more than four million followers.

In 1928 we received a visit from the American Unitarian Rev. Dr. John Lathrop. He took a great interest in our work and relayed our story back to the leadership of the Unitarian Church in Boston. In 1931 both de los Reyes and I were invited to the United States to visit Unitarian Churches and for me to receive an honorary doctorate from Meadville Theological School.

In the following years we sought a close relationship with the American Unitarians, since our basic beliefs were so closely allied. We were Unitarians in every way other than official affiliation. We did all we could to interest the AUA, but received little but a courteous hearing. The answer was always, "Let's wait and see how things develop."

My earthly life ended in 1940. The Japanese invaded and occupied our land in 1941. By the time the war was over much that we had built over the previous four decades was in shambles.

De los Reyes' son assumed leadership of the Independent Church, adopted a Trinitarian Declaration of Faith and eventually merged with the Episcopal Church of the Philippines.

One can only wonder how differently it might have turned out had the American Unitarians been more responsive to our overtures for union.

But truth cannot be so easily defeated. Beaten to the earth in one place it springs forth and blossoms in another. But how Universalism arose from a most unusual source and remains vibrant in the Philippines is another story, better told by another person.

Good Morning. I am

TORIBIO QUIMADA

I am the founder of the Universalist Church in the Philippines.

It would have been impossible to predict that would be my role in life considering my difficult beginnings. I was next to the oldest of the thirteen children of poor parents. My father was a carpenter and also added to his income by farming. We did not have much in the way of worldly goods, but we were a family of great love for one another.

We were Catholics, and I frequently heard my parents discussing religious matters. I heard them criticize the Bible, for we were taught by the priests that it was a fraudulent book written by the arch-heretic Martin Luther. I was curious, and wished to see a Bible and read it for myself, but that was forbidden by the Church.

Then, in 1935, during the Great Depression we were forced to leave our native Cebu Province and move to Nataban, San Carlos City. My uncle, a brother of my father, was a Protestant leader in that area, and for the first time I became acquainted with many people of the Protestant faith.

My Uncle Fernando gave me a Protestant Bible and I read it and studied it with great enthusiasm. Though I remained a Catholic, I began to attend Protestant services and Sunday School, where I asked many questions and engaged in lengthy discussions. Many of the members thought I was attending only to criticize them, but my true purpose was to learn.

After a while they came to understand that I was seeking knowledge and understanding by my persistent questioning, and they accepted me. In fact, I was asked to teach Sunday School and even to preach sermons on occasions when the minister was away.

In 1943, while the Philippines were occupied by the Japanese in World War II, my family and I were baptized in the Protestant Church. Even my father, who had earlier been so critical, joined me as a member of the *Iglesia Universal de Christo*, the Universal Church of Christ, as we were called.

Five years later the General Minister of the Church gave his permission for me to be ordained as minister of a newly organized congregation in Navididan, Prosperidad, San Carlos City. This was an overwhelming responsibility for me, particularly because I had only an elementary school education. I had not attended high school because it was necessary for me to work and help support our family. But I threw myself wholeheartedly into the work, trusting God to see me through.

We were a very poor congregation and in great need of Bibles, hymnbooks, and Sunday School educational materials. I appealed for help to all the denominations in the Philippines, but to no avail. Then I found a directory of churches in America. I looked under the letter "U", hoping to find *Iglesia Universal de Kristo*. Instead I found a listing for the Universalist Church in Gloucester, Massachusetts.

The minister there, Rev. Carl Westman, wrote back expressing his surprise that there was a Universalist Church in the Philippines. He put me in touch with the Universalist Service Committee, who sent us all kinds of educational materials, which we gladly put to use.

This infuriated the leaders of our Filipino denomination, and they expelled me from the ministry and took away all my credentials. What might have been a great tragedy in my life turned into a glorious blessing. The Universalist denomination in America accepted my congregation into their association, and helped in getting the Universalist Church of the Philippines registered as an official body with our government.

They also made it possible for me to receive further education. First, it was arranged for me to take an examination which would serve in lieu of a high school diploma and permit me to enter college. But it had been so long since I had attended any school, I failed the exam. They did not give up on me, however, and I did not give up on myself. I enrolled in the Calatrava Public High School, graduated in two years, and continued immediately at Foundation University in Dumaguete City. During all this period the Universalist Association covered all expenses for me and my family.

By the time I had completed my degree the Universalists and the Unitarians in America had merged and our church became the Unitarian Universalist Church of the Philippines.

At this time I chose not to return to Nataban which was a great distance and quite inaccessible except by horseback. Rather I purchased a plot of ground nearer the city where we established a headquarters for our growing network of small congregations.

In addition to my preaching and teaching, I also felt it necessary to apply the religious principles of love and compassion to society outside the church. This led me into a leadership role in the struggle for land reform in behalf of the impoverished farmers. On a number of occasions I was told by the authorities that I must desist from these efforts, but that I could not do. I could not preach about a God whose love was infinite while standing aside and seeing God's children starve to fill the coffers of the wealthy landowners.

At the same time, 1988, I was overjoyed to receive word that our application for membership in the Unitarian Universalist Association had been approved. I was invited to go to America and be officially recognized at the General Assembly. That would have been a crowning glory to a life filled with unexpected pleasures and opportunities.

But it was not to be. The threats against me had grown more intense and I had been ordered to stop my efforts in behalf of the poor. Of course, I had refused. In May 1988, only weeks before my scheduled trip to America I was gunned down by government troops. My body was carried inside and my house was burned to the ground.

Two others attended the General Assembly in my stead.

Our work continues on and on.

Good Morning. I am

REBECCA QUIMADA-SIENES

The murder of my beloved father, founder of the Universalist Church of the Philippines, left me in deep despair. Even the privilege of posthumously representing him at the General Assembly, when our church was officially accepted into fellowship with the American Unitarian Universalist Association, was a bittersweet experience.

The fog which had descended on my spirit only began to lift three years later when I was admitted to Meadville/Lombard Seminary in Chicago. That gave me renewed hope that I would be able to carry on the work my father had begun.

I was one of those people Derrick Bell has called "faces at the bottom of the well." A poor woman from an impoverished country with little education . . . desperate and frustrated with life. Out of hopelessness, I sighed, Is there a God? If there is, why is that God unjust, unkind, unmerciful to my sufferings and the sufferings of my people? Why isn't God fair? Why does all the good fortune fall into the hands of those who are already rich? Why do poor people lose their jobs or their lives if they seek fairness, justice, and equality? Why do the wealthy have land, while the poor have only debts? These were the questions I took with me as I embarked on my theological studies.

It is a paradox that I had to go to America to learn how to be a true servant of the Philippines. My studies of liberation theology gave me insight into my own situation and the mission to which I must dedicate my life.

I learned that I must uphold my roots and my heritage; that I must nourish my own indigenous tradition; that I must contextualize my theology. I came home committed to being an organic catalyst, an involved participant, and a leader in my struggling community.

The majority of the members of the Unitarian Universalist Church of the Philippines are farmers and fishermen. We belong to the lowest rung of the economic ladder in our society. I am outraged that the poor are always labeled as beggars, dirty, illiterates, useless human beings, and a burden to society.

I am saddened that just as poor people are considered eyesores to society, we poor Unitarian Universalists in the Philippines seem to be considered eyesores to our denomination—a movement widely known for its wealthy, elitist, professional and intellectual membership. That stigma has a powerful impact on our religious leadership, and we are just beginning to learn how to use it to our own advantage.

The gospel of universal salvation preached by my father was a liberating and transformative agent in the lives of poor Filipinos. We, the poor, foresee the resurrection of Jesus as our emancipation from the bondage of oppression. We anticipate the day when we shall break loose from the shackles of exploitation we have long suffered at the hands of first world countries and the hands of our own wealthy elite Filipinos.

The missionary efforts of my father in bringing this liberating vision to the oppressed Filipinos, and the shedding of his innocent blood in behalf of his faith, have firmly focused my commitment to continuing his noble work.

It is my personal covenant to nourish that seed of Universalism that he sowed in the Philippines and to establish a written record of his work in the history of Unitarian Universalism. I will not permit it to be forgotten.

We have so many bright, talented children. Boys and girls who can become future leaders of our church and our society. We have ways of improving our standards of living. The lack of resources, however, suppresses the talents of our children and hinders our ability to improve our livelihood. It is my personal covenant to establish literacy and economic programs for our church. I am determined to seek funding from interested UU churches and members around the world to make it possible for our young people to receive quality university educations.

We are currently engaged in a credit cooperative program. Through a grant from the International Association for Religious Freedom we have established a credit union, which provides loans to improve the livelihood of our members. We help farmers buy fertilizer, provide capital for small business enterprises, and buy fishing equipment for fishermen.

Most recently an international UU funding panel has given us a grant to plant a mango farm. In a few years, when the trees are mature, they will provide resources for many other developmental programs, which will benefit all.

Liberation theologian Gustavo Gutierez has written: "To be poor means to die of hunger, to be exploited with others, not to know that you are being exploited, not to know that you are a person."

We Unitarian Universalists of the Philippines are still poor, but we are learning to know that we are persons. Persons of value! Persons worthy of dignity and respect! Persons destined for higher and better things! We are determined, together, to fulfill our promise and claim our rightful destiny as sons and daughters of God.

Just a few years ago I never dreamed I would end up preaching sermons, leading worship, giving lectures, sharing this kind of personal covenant, or serving as the elected leader of a national church.

But that is who I have become. How that transformation from the dispirited, frightened, lonely, heartbroken, displaced woman who arrived at Meadville just a decade ago, to the confident, committed person I am today is surely a miracle of grace.

May I close with a song? A simple little song that means so very much to me. I know you know it, too. It is the essence of my Credo.

> "This little light of mine,
> I'm gonna let it shine . . .
>
> All over the world. . .
>
> Bringing light to all . . .
>
> This little light of mine,
> Let it shine. Let it shine.
> Let it shine."

Good Morning. I am

INDERIAS DOMINIC BHATTI

I am the founder and leader of the Unitarian community in Pakistan.

I was born in 1963 in Gojra, District Fasialabad, Punjab, Pakistan. My father was Headmaster of a Catholic school. I was raised in the school compound, which included quarters for teachers, a hostel for students and houses for the priests. One priest was principal of the school.

Since I was the son of the Headmaster I was highly honored by the other school boys. Many Muslims and Protestants were among my closest friends. In sharing our mutual childhood concerns we learned of the sexual abuse of one boy in the hostel. Under the guise of needing extra tutoring for studies in which he was weak, he was abused many times by one of the priests. This boy told one of the Muslim students what had been done to him, and that student reported it on to me. After this a number of the boys—most of them my close friends—protested the atrocious conduct.

As a result my father was dismissed as Headmaster and transferred to another school in the village of Khushpur.

This was the point at which I first began to question the morality and authority of the Church. I had seen its hypocrisy and misuse of power at close range.

That, however, did not keep me from preparing for my Confirmation. But as I studied I wrestled with further doubts on a number of issues. Among them:

1. The idea of the Trinity
2. Grace and Blessing through Mother Mary
3. Priests as the models of Christ
4. Only communicants of the Church are holy and acceptable to God.

When I found the courage to express these doubts I was subjected to beatings with a stick by my Catechism instructor for questioning the Divine Mysteries and Dogmas. Further, I was isolated from my Muslim and Protestant friends. The priests said I had been corrupted by these evil enemies of the True Church.

At age 16, I entered Sialkot Murray College. Very shortly after this my mother died, and my father soon re-married. My step-mother suggested to my father that it would be better for me to be in a teacher training school rather than an expensive college. He agreed and my financial support was ended.

Many of my Protestant and Muslim friends rallied to my aid. One missionary, a Miss Nickle, reviewed my academic record and agreed to sponsor my college expenses, including a monthly stipend of 100 Rupees for pocket money. This was a most generous offer, but due to a sense of family obligation, I felt it necessary to leave college as my father had asked.

I took a position as an untrained primary schoolteacher, supporting myself as well as giving part of my income to my family.

Under pressure from family and the Catholic Missionaries who cared for the support of my two younger sisters, I agreed to enter the seminary. I studied there for the next five years. During that time I developed a strong interest in Liberation Theology, which taught that God primarily stood with the poor and the oppressed and against the wealthy and tyrannical. I was greatly impressed by the teachings of the progressive Catholic leaders to which I was exposed.

During my seminary studies I wrote two major papers, each more than fifty typewritten pages in length.

The first was on the notion of the evil spirit. I said that traditional teaching of an evil spirit working in the world was the cause of many phobias among the faithful. I concluded that a true religion should be a liberating force in life rather than a cause of tension, guilt, fear and sense of sinfulness.

The second major paper was a critical analysis of the rule of celibacy for members of the clergy. As a result of this thesis I was advised to leave the seminary.

With the support and backing of a number of liberal Catholics I was employed by Caritas Pakistan, a social service organization sponsored by the Conference of Bishops. It was a good program, designed to be a genuine service to the common people. It helped people live in a way consistent with Christian principles.

After only three years, however, my liberal and progressive approach proved more than the Bishops could endure. I was forced to resign. Those who stood beside me and protested my removal were branded heretics, atheists, and the Anti-Christ. Slowly I became their untitled priest.

We were bound together by a sharing of the following principles:

1. God the creator of the universe.
2. Christ a human who found divinity within himself.
3. Every human born with the togetherness of male and female.
4. No inherited sin.
5. Every human with potential of growth, nobility, divine character and wisdom.
6. No eternal punishment.
7. Love of God is equal for all.

In 1991 I found a reference to Unitarianism in a dictionary of religions. It described exactly the ideas my friends and I had developed on our own. We organized as a Unitarian Church and in 1994 became a member of the International Council of Unitarians and Universalists.

We seek to promote justice, peace, and human dignity. We offer therapy to socio-religiously confused and disturbed people. We work with people for social, economic, cultural and religious attitudinal change at the individual, family and community levels. Ultimately, we strive toward religious liberalism and social justice to the accessless, resourceless and demoralized people of Pakistan.

Bom Dia! Eu sou

PAULO I. ERENO

I was born into a very poor family in the extreme south of Brazil. I am now a Unitarian, but I traveled a long and circuitous route to arrive at this place. My mother was a Catholic, but not much of a church-going one. My father was a free-thinker. My brothers and sisters and I were encouraged from the beginning to seek our own way.

When I was 11 I considered myself a Methodist. Then I studied in a 7th Day Adventist boarding school. Before long I grew disappointed by what I considered their fanaticism and intolerance, so I left school and found a job. My spiritual pilgrimage was just beginning.

The journey took me through Spiritualism, Theosophy, the Rosicrucians and other forms of occultism. But none of them were fully satisfying to me. I found too much preoccupation with the invisible, the other worlds and dimensions, the afterlife, the unseen; and a remarkable lack of concern for the here and now.

Please don't misunderstand me. I never officially disowned any of those just mentioned. I am still bound by my vows to respect them. They are all good organizations which do much to spread knowledge and insight about religion and philosophy. And, of course, there are plenty of good people in them. It is simply that I opted for something more down to earth!

When I was 24 years old, that was in 1973, I left Brazil and moved to Holland to work in the international headquarters of the Esperanto Movement. I met another Esperantist who was a Unitarian lay preacher and gave me my introduction to this approach to life which I have adopted as my own.

But it was not a sudden conversion. I went to London to study Buddhism, and have been left with the appreciation of that way that nourishes my soul to this day.

My first reaction to Unitarianism, as it was described to me, was bafflement over the "teachings of a religion without any teachings." But the more I read, heard, and searched inwardly, the more I understood, and the more my enthusiasm grew.

The English minister, Rev. Frank Walker of Cambridge Unitarian Church summarized my Credo in one of his sermons: "The point is to find inner harmony, and to be able to give this inner harmony some social expression, refraining all the while to impose our views on others."

That captures the essence of my religious thought. For me religion is basically finding inner harmony. That is, finding peace within ourselves and finding ways to spread this peace around us.

I don't deny anyone else's need for something of a more transcendental nature. It only means that, as a Unitarian, it is not up to me to impose any transcendental value on others. They will have to elaborate their own values and beliefs—be it Yoga, Zen-Buddhism, or whatever.

Since returning to my native Brazil in 1981 I have tried to establish a beachhead for Unitarianism here. It has not been an easy task. We are a poor country and the daily struggle for survival is a time-consuming and energy-depleting challenge.

I find many who are sympathetic to our Unitarian Universalist views, but too often they say, "If I believe in freedom, why tie myself down to a group of any kind?"

Little by little we are establishing a network across the South American continent. Our Temple is the internet, our fellowship is through e-mail. But we do not give up. The task is too important.

Another thing I want to explore is the possibility of establishing a community where people can work together and share the results of their work in more just and environmentally friendly ways. I have been impressed by the fact that many Unitarians in the past tried to build such cooperative communities. I think the idea is still valid, and in time I plan to raise that flag.

Let me finish by quoting from a letter I wrote to my co-religionist brothers and sisters in India: "Being a Unitarian is like having a chunk of heaven inside of oneself. When I am suffering I remember I am a Unitarian, and no amount of suffering is enough to break down my resolve. I want to be a Unitarian for as long as I live, and just in case there is any such thing as reincarnation, I want to be a Unitarian in all my future lives, and even after that!"

I hardly ever pray, but I do meditate. I also like to recite mantras once in a while. I have found one that is very powerful in my case, and gives me lots of strength and encouragement in all circumstances of life:

I AM A UNITARIAN!

Buenas Dias. Soy

OLGA BEATRIZ FLORES BEDREGAL

I am part of a small, but highly motivated, group of seekers in La Paz, Bolivia who are engaged in the creation of what we consider to be a new resource and new vision of Unitarian Universalism.

We are striving to find a harmonious blending of our indigenous Andean spirituality with the traditional Unitarian rationalism.

This new creation begins with revalorization and rescantando—that is, in English, reevaluating and rescuing—our indigenous vision of the cosmos. We draw strength from the majestic mountains which surround us. We perceive divinity in every living thing. This is similar to, but more far-reaching, I believe, than the seventh principle of the American UU association which affirms "respect for the interdependent web of all existence, of which we are a part."

This inspires us to political action as an expression of ethical behavior essential to finding a solution of the tragic injustices which pollute our society.

We are developing an approach that combines the mystical return to our Mother Land—Pachamama—and the good expressions of globalization we find manifested in Unitarian Universalism.

Our roots are neither Unitarian nor Universalist, and yet we are a Latin American version of both. Our people have a long history of religious syncretism and this is an expression of that ability to extract the best from other traditions and blend them into a unitary new reality.

You might gain insight into our quest by viewing the painting of Juan Carlos Achata, one of Bolivia's finest artists, and a member

245

of our group. He is a surrealist who uses bold and imaginative colors. His paintings are abstract and spiritually influenced, such as a watchful eye looking over landscapes. To view his interpretative representation of Illimanti, the guardian mountain of La Paz, is to look deeply into the soul of our movement.

But do not be misled into thinking that this esthetic appreciation of the natural world has shielded us from the real and pressing problems of the world in which we live. Nothing could be farther from the truth.

Our movement has arisen out of our common reflection on the great issues we face in our time: deterioration of the environment, over population, rampant nationalism, over production, and the great disparity of income between the rich and the poor.

These problems are physical realities, but the crisis is in the sphere of the spirit. We struggle for the soul of humankind.

Modern man's obsession with the accumulation of things has resulted in an ethical degrading of law that poisons our era. Our emphasis on that which is pragmatic rather than what is fair and just, has distorted our conduct.

These problems will not be solved by conventional ways of thinking and acting. They will only be solved with a global change of life, based on new mental structures which can comprehend subtle realities which now elude our thought processes.

Only when we recognize that there is another reality than the one which is visible will the new global philosophy arise which can lift the human family from its current state.

It seems apparent that we may soon be saturated by science, technology, consumerism and power politics. The inevitable result will be catastrophic. Even the evangelicals with their fervent preaching about an approaching apocalypse are going unheard because capitalism has removed us so far from God that we have lost any sense of our divine essence.

Consumerism is reducing the human species to a commodity, like meat, buyable and negotiable. This is slowly killing our sense of the esthetic, the ethical, and the transcendent realities.

Before we all suffocate, before it is too late, a religious wave must arise to restore to mankind its conscience. Only when we, the members of the human family, comprehend that there are realities other than capital and profit will we be able to pull ourselves from the current abyss.

I learned most of what I currently believe from my mother, Carmen Bedregal de Flores, director of the School of Social Work at a university. Raised a Catholic, mother was a living demonstration that one did not have to go to the convent to be religious. Her faith was one that brought ethical insight into the everyday events of life. Not surprisingly, the fact that she took the teachings of Jesus so seriously and challenged the society around her to do the same, she was deemed to be a radical by defenders of the status quo.

When I was a child, mother instituted a campaign against world hunger right in our home. We were encouraged to eat simply and sparingly in empathetic identification with the starving children of Africa. In one way our efforts were a failure. We did not solve the problem of world hunger. But in another way it succeeded beyond all expectations. We brought the problems of the world right to our family table. I have been left, many years later, with a continuing determination to challenge the religious people of the world to actually share with the hungry. Just think what we might do!

Mother identified strongly with the Virgin Mary, not in a theological or creedal sense, but as an expression of the "feminine face of God." This is another of her contributions to our emerging Unitarian Universalism in Bolivia.

She lived her philosophy of life. She didn't preach it. She lived it. I do not remember her saying, "Take up your cross and follow," but I saw her do it time and time again.

Unitarian Universalism in Latin America has many sources. What I learned from my mother are among the concepts which I am striving to incorporate into the life of our religious community.

Let those who have eyes behold our vision! Let those who have ears listen to our song!

Books, Articles and Web Sites

A major source of information for this book has been the Unitarian Universalist Biographical Dictionary, which is an artesian well of information for anyone interested in the history of this liberal religious movement. Click on www.uua.org/uuhs/duub for almost everything you ever wanted to know on this subject. My thanks to chief editor, Peter Hughes.

Another Internet gold mine has been <u>Our Unitarian Heritage</u>, by Earl Morse Wilbur which is available on-line from Starr King School Ministry. This provides a comprehensive history from 160 C.E. to 1925 when this book was published.
http://online.sksm.edu/ouh

Other sources from which I have engaged in benign literary larceny are:

A sermon <u>"Carpathian Orchids and Dandelions"</u> by Rev. Dr. Judith A. Walker.

A sermon <u>"Not To Think Alike But To Love Alike: A Visit from Francis David"</u> by the Rev. Michael McGee, Arlington, VA, 2000.

<u>"The Right to Heresy, Castellio Against Calvin"</u>, by Stefan Zweig, 1951.

<u>"Norbert Fabian Capek: A Spiritual Journey"</u>, by Richard Henry, 1999.

<u>"Unitarians in Canada"</u>, by Phillip Hewett, Canadian Unitarian Council, 1978.

<u>"Wanted: A Single Canada"</u>, by J. T. Thorson, McClelland & Stewart, 1973.

<u>"Maglipay Universalist"</u>, by Fredric John Muir, Annapolis, MD, 2001.

<u>"Unitarians and India"</u>, by Spencer Lavan, Exploration Press, 1991.

"Mary Carpenter in India", Norman Sargant, Bristol, UK 1987.

"I Am Not A Missionary - Margaret Barr in India", Kairos Winter, 1983.

"Song of the Waterfall", by Elizabeth Kyle, Holt, Rinehart, Winston, 1970.

"Joseph Priestley: A Comet in the System", by John Ruskin Clark, 1990.

"Memoirs of Dr. Joseph Priestley", edited by John T. Boyer, 1964.

"Josiah Wedgwood: A Biography", Anthony Burton, 1976.

"Mary Wollstonecraft: A Revolutionary Life", by Janet Todd, 2000.

"Unbridling the Tongues of Women", by Susan Magarey, Hale & Iremonger, 1985.

"The Halway House to Infidelity", by Dorothy Scott, Unitarian Fellowship of Australia, 1980.

"Are We, Even Today, Socinians?", by George Beach.

"Truth in a Heresy", by Leonard Smith, Unitarian College, Manchester.

"Faustus Socinius", by Zbigniew Ogonowski.

"For Faith and Freedom: Short History of Unitarianism in Europe", Charles Howe.

"The Unitarians of South Africa—A Socio-Historical Study", doctoral thesis of Eric Heller-Wagner, University of Stellenbosch, 1995.

For additional information on most of the personalities featured in this book check the Internet. It is absolutely amazing what you can find there. Here are a few of the sites I found most helpful.

A Liberal Religious Heritage
www.hibbert.org.uk/heritage/history

Women Making History
www.csmonitor.com

Judith Sargent Murray
http://home.att.net/-uusnews/murray

Conversion of John Murray
http://uua.org/uucj/jmur

Life and Trance of Dr. George de Benneville
www.athens.net

Dorothy Livesay - Interview
www.uuottawa.com/livesay

Canadian Unitarians and Universalists
www.euc.ca/who we are/short history.htm

Emily Jennings Stowe
www.nle-bnc.ca/2/12/h 12-207-e.html

Canadian Unitarianism and Universalism
www.uuottawa.com/cul 1.html

Vilhjalmur Steffanson: Arctic Explorer
www.harvardsquarelibrary.org

Australian Dictionary of Biography
abd@coombs.anu.edu.au

Female Firebrands and Reformers
www.Geocities.com

A Celebration of Women Writers
http://digital.library.upenn.edu

National Archives Learning Curve
www.spartacus.schoolnet.co.uk

Life and Reforms of Raja Ram Mohun Roy Bahadoor
http://campross.freeyellow.com

Unitarian Universalist Involvement in India, John Buehrens
Uua.org/re/reach/fall00